"IT WAS AN AWFUL EXPERIENCE . . ."

Again, he was put in a room with no windows and about 20 people, in relays, continued "the same treatment, calling me anti-Semitic, a Nazi. They showed pictures of the holocaust, screaming that I had betrayed my own people."

"They'd rip up copies of New Testaments in front of my face and throw it at me, stuff pieces in my ears and mouth and burn them. Every time I went to sleep they'd wake me up. It went on all week."

KIDNAPPED FOR MY FAITH

Ken Levitt with Ceil Rosen

Published by Bible Voice, Inc.
P.O. Box 7491
Van Nuys, CA 91409

Preface

...I said, My strength and my hope is perished from the LORD.

Remembering mine affliction and my misery, the wormwood and the gall.

My soul hath them still in remembrance, and is humbled in me.

This I recall to my mind, therefore have I hope.

It is of the LORD's mercies that we are not consumed, because his compassions fail not.

They are new every morning: great is thy faithfulness.

The LORD is my portion, saith my soul; therefore will I hope in him.

(Lamentations 3:18-24)

Chapter 1
Kidnapped

Thursday, May 18, 1978 was a day I'll never forget. The early evening air pressed in warm and muggy through the car windows, and conflicting emotions of hope and apprehension fought for control of my thoughts as I wound through the familiar streets of Newton, Massachusetts, the Jewish community where I grew up. After the siege of spring rains, it was good to see the sun. Its last rays highlighted the comfortable homes and well-manicured lawns, glinting off of picture windows and cars parked in broad driveways. Saplings, planted only twelve years earlier when my family first moved there, had finally earned the right to be called trees. Now they cast long shadows with their froth of budding greenery. The neighborhood at dinner was quiet. That pleasant, peaceful scene held a promise of long sunny days to come, but I wasn't feeling very tranquil as I steered my old Ford Maverick into the cul de sac where my parents lived.

On the dashboard shelf next to my pocket Bible lay some important documents. They were marriage licenses, issued by Middlesex County, Commonwealth of Massachusetts, to Christine Cox and Kenneth Levitt. Well, maybe Middlesex County sanctioned my marriage to Christine next Sunday, but my parents, Mildred and Al Levitt, certainly didn't approve. They had made this all too plain to both Christine and me on numerous occasions, and their bitter, unrelenting attitude over this and over my two-year-old faith in Christ had put an almost unbearable strain on my relationship with them.

Three days earlier, my father had telephoned me. His conciliatory tone surprised me and gave me new hope.

"Ken," he began, "I haven't seen you for a while. I'd like to speak to you once more before you go away for two weeks on Sunday. Besides, I want to give you the rest of the money I owe you from those stock sales I handled for you.

Why don't you come over to the house tomorrow night? We'll talk."

I hesitated. He knew that Tuesday was my regular Bible study night, and was always trying to arrange conflicting schedules so I would miss going.

"No, I can't tomorrow. I'm busy."

"Can't it wait?" he countered.

"No."

"Well, how about Wednesday night at eight?"

I hesitated again. "I can't at eight. I'm busy then, too. Why does it have to be at eight? I'll come over at five."

His voice was tense. "No, I can't see you at five. We're taking a trip this weekend, I have to get the car in shape, and I have an appointment at the garage. It can't be changed."

I thought for a minute. "How about Thursday?"

"O.K.," he said. "Thursday at eight."

"No, not at eight. I can't." I remembered that was the time for our wedding rehearsal. "How about four o'clock?" I asked.

He sounded even more upset. I couldn't figure out why the time was so important. Finally, we agreed I would try to come on Thursday at 6:30, but I couldn't stay more than an hour because of the rehearsal.

Thursday morning my mother came to see me at my new apartment in Newtonville. I was doing some chores, getting it ready for Chris and me to move in after the wedding.

My mother wouldn't come inside. She stayed outside and talked to me through the window.

"I've been worried about you, Ken. I kept calling your house in Waltham for two days, and you didn't answer."

"I've been sleeping over here, Ma. There are so many last minute things to do. Come on in."

She insisted on staying outside. It was as though she couldn't bear to see where Christine and I would be living together.

"I just wanted to make sure you were coming over tonight. Come for dinner. Six-thirty." She seemed agitated and avoided my eyes as she spoke.

"Oh, and bring your guitar. Your sister asked to look at it because she's thinking of buying one and wants to compare styles and sizes."

"O.K., Ma, see you later." I shook my head as she turned and left. She was generally a rather nervous person, but today she seemed worse than usual. Maybe it was the strain of my approaching wedding that had set her off.

Remembering these things now, I sighed as I slowed down in front of my parents' green and white split level. I hoped that we could have a pleasant visit together. The driveway was empty. Where were their cars? Could they have forgotten about my visit and gone off somewhere? Mom had made such a point of my coming over tonight. I shrugged. Might as well park in the driveway, since there was room. The drapes were all shut, too. How odd! They had to be home.

As I walked up the path to the house, I prayed quickly that God would bless this visit and make it a time for healing our bruised relationship. I fished for my old key, unaware that within minutes I would be embarking on the most bizarre experience of my life.

Propping the storm door open with my guitar, I turned the key easily in the familiar lock. I set the guitar down in the foyer and looked around. It was dark inside.

Then I saw my father standing at the top of the short staircase leading to the living room. I wondered why he looked so nervous.

"Hi, Dad."

"Hi, Kenny. How are you doing?" he asked.

"Fine, glad to see you. Where ... ?" I heard scuffling noises behind me. Before I could turn around, someone tackled me and wrestled me to the floor, face down. Another person twisted my arms in back of me and grabbed me under the chin. I managed to bite his hand before he got my head in a viselike grip inside his elbow. I fought hard, but they were too strong for me. Hands were tugging a cloth of some kind over my head, tying me up, dragging me in the direction of the attached garage. Heart pounding from shock and the effort of my struggles, I could hardly breathe.

"Dad," I gasped, "why are you doing this?"

His voice shook with emotion. "Do what they want, and everything will be all right."

I certainly didn't want to do what they wanted, whoever "they" were. I just wanted to get away. As I continued to struggle, my captors grew rougher.

"Stop fighting if you know what's good for you," one snarled. "You'd better cooperate, or we'll break you head! Will you come quietly, or do we have to knock you out?"

I heard my father's voice in the background. "Don't hurt him."

We were in the garage, and they were shoving me inside a car. From the height and position of the doors, I could tell it was a van or truck of some kind. They threw me down, covered me with a blanket, and two people sat on me. I heard my father getting in, too. I tried to move, but couldn't.

"You'd better be quiet," a voice growled.

"I'm suffocating with this thing over my face," I panted, "and whatever you've got me tied with is cutting into my wrists and ankles!"

"Aw, he's just lying," one said.

My father sounded concerned. Again he instructed, "Don't hurt him, don't hurt him! Loosen the ties a little. Give him some fresh air."

They opened the window a crack more and loosened the ties on my wrists, but they wouldn't remove the hood.

The van moved out of the garage and down the streets, picking up speed as it came to a major highway. Pinned down by those two heavy bodies, bruised, angry and frightened, I couldn't imagine where they were taking me, or what they would do. There was only one thing I could do. I prayed.

Chapter 2

Good Boys Don't Believe in Jesus

Kidnapped and tortured for my faith! It sounds unreal in this modern age of supposed enlightenment, like a page out of the Book of Acts. Some people might find my story hard to believe. But I know it happened. The memories of those two weeks—the hardships, terror and final escape are indelibly etched on my mind. And if I should ever begin to forget, I have a broken nose as a permanent reminder.

In order for those outside of the Jewish community to understand how such an incredible thing could happen to me, I must first describe the conflicts and anguish of soul, and the reactions of the Jewish people who confront a Jewish person who contemplates believing in Jesus. The Jewish community is programmed by rabbinic tradition never to consider belief in Jesus as an option. Frightened and defensive because of centuries of anti-Semitic persecutions, many Jewish people regard Christianity with suspicion and look upon any Jewish believer in Christ as a traitor or *meshumad*, one who destroys himself.

In all fairness, I must state that this suspicion and negative attitude toward Christianity doesn't usually result in the kind of treatment I suffered. Most Jewish people abhor violence and strong-arm tactics. We've endured too much of that ourselves at the hands of Hamans, Hitlers, and Inquisitors down through the ages. The people who abducted me and held me prisoner represent a very small, misguided segment of the Jewish community. Most Jewish people wouldn't stoop to such methods, however much they might disagree with a fellow Jew's beliefs and religious commitments. Nevertheless, when I, a Jew, accepted Christ as my Savior in July of 1976, I knew I would face severe problems with my family and friends. I also knew that God had revealed His truth to me, and I dared not refuse it, no matter what the consequences might be.

Looking back, I see that my conservative Jewish background must have influenced my ultimate decision to follow Christ. Though for several years during my late teens I fell away from the Judaism of my youth and tried to ignore all thoughts of God, the seeds of faith remained.

From the time I was old enough to read, my parents sent me to an orthodox Jewish Hebrew school in Natick. For six years, I sat three afternoons a week in that classroom, learning Hebrew, Torah* and Jewish customs.

My mother kept a kosher house. That meant we observed all the dietary restrictions prescribed in the Law of Moses. We ate no pork or shellfish, and didn't mix meat with dairy products. My parents also observed the Sabbath to the best of their ability, by doing no work, kindling no fire, riding in no vehicle, handling no money, from sunset Friday night until sunset Saturday night. And they taught these precepts to their children.

When I was thirteen years old, my father's climb up the ladder of success brought us to Newton, a somewhat better neighborhood in the greater Boston area. My family continued to observe Judaism, but some of the more stringent aspects fell by the wayside at that time. We no longer lived within walking distance of a synagogue, and it became necessary to ride to services, which is regarded as a sin by the very orthodox Jews. Still, my parents tried their best to maintain Jewish discipline. They carefully impressed upon me and my younger brother and sister the absolute necessity of keeping our associations and social life strictly within the Jewish community. They kept a tight rein on us and frowned on anything more than a most casual relationship with Gentiles.

Along with the standard admonitions that a good boy is kind to his parents, does well in school, and keeps his room clean, I learned that a good boy doesn't grow up and marry a Gentile, and a good boy never believes in Jesus, the Gentile god.

---

* Torah refers to Pentateuch, the Law of Moses.

During my summers, I went to an orthodox Jewish camp situated in a lush green area of New Hampshire. There, at Camp Yavneh, we spoke Hebrew rather than English. We recited lengthy morning prayers every day and said Hebrew benedictions before and after each strictly kosher meal. Along with the usual crafts classes associated with summer camps, we had lessons in religion before they turned us loose to swim, play ball, hike and do all those things kids do at summer camp.

When I finished the first six years of Hebrew school, I was about twelve years old. That was the year I studied for my bar mitzvah, the special confirmation service for all Jewish boys when they reach the age of thirteen. At that time I took on in theory, if not in practice, all the obligations of the Law of Moses. I then went on to another Jewish school of higher learning. This Hebrew "college" was affiliated with Camp Yavneh where I had been spending my summers. It continued where the other school left off, with more advanced courses in Hebrew, Old Testament, and rabbinic commentary. Unfortunately, all this intensive training didn't foster in me any real zeal for God. The older I got, the less interested I became in Judaism.

When I passed the age for being a camper, I continued at Camp Yavneh as a counsellor in training. It was during one of our nightly discussions in the bunk house one summer that I finally admitted to myself that maybe I didn't believe in God any more. Some of the other boys in the bunk were saying that they didn't believe that God was anything more than a man-made idea, because people had to believe in something. He was just a concept of faith, rather than a real person. That made sense to me. I felt I was too "scientific" to believe in the God and religion of my childhood now that I was growing up.

After high school, I enrolled at Boston University. I didn't know what I wanted to do, but everyone in my peer group was expected to go to college, so I went, too. But I didn't care enough to study much. As my unbelief in God and disenchantment with the world around me grew, so did my impatience with school. Lacking motivation, I let my grades slide to the point of no return. Finally, I flunked out.

By then I was thoroughly disillusioned about my earlier religious training. I felt that if God were alive at all, He was the Creator of all people, not just the Jewish God, and that He loved all men equally. Also, for the first time since I was thirteen and my family moved to Newton, I developed friendships with Gentiles. I rebelled at the exclusivism I had been taught at home, that idea that Jews should only relate to other Jews. I know now that my parents stressed this way of life because they were defensive and afraid of losing their children to the non-Jewish world. But then I couldn't deal with it, nor did I care to try.

I was disillusioned, too, about the absurdity of life in general. I thought if there was a God, He must be up there somewhere laughing at the mess men made of their lives. I felt that all religions were man-made rather than God-given because they built up so many walls between people. If there really was a God, I thought, He wouldn't want all these man-made walls that divide us.

I also worried about death. If there was no God, if there was no after-life, what happened to a person when he died? What physical part of a human being was the real substance of that personality? What happened at death? Was it total instantaneous annihilation, or some horrible, slow disintegration of being?

All these things disturbed me. I didn't believe in God, and yet part of me did believe. I hoped there was Somebody up there, even while my intellect told me that it wasn't possible.

Sometimes, when things were going well for me, I prayed, almost superstitiously, just in case Somebody was listening. For the most part, all that I could readily admit was that there might be some creative Force or Energy, but God probably wasn't a personal being who cared for or responded to people's needs. That was my frame of mind when my old friend Steve started me on the train of thought that changed my life.

Chapter 3

Is Somebody Out There?

> Who hath ascended up into heaven, or descended? Who hath gathered the wind in his fists? Who hath bound the waters in a garment? Who hath established all the ends of the earth? What is his name and what is his son's name, if thou canst tell? (Proverbs 30:4)

The early spring air was refreshingly brisk as Steve and I pitched our tent. Good friends since our early teens, we both had a passion for camping out and many interests in common. There was plenty of time to talk and philosophize as we finished setting up our campsite in the White Mountain National Forest. We could see snow on the higher elevations and a full stream rushed past the grove of trees that lined the clearing we chose. The area was perfect and serene. As we enjoyed the natural beauty of the place, we discussed ecology.

"I wonder if all this stuff will still be here ten years from now," Steve mused.

I shrugged. "Probably not, the way things are going these days. Someone will come along and chop down the trees, or maybe carelessness will start a forest fire and destroy everything. Natural beauty is fast becoming a thing of the past. It'll never be replaced."

From man's destructive nature, the conversation turned to speculation about a higher power behind "nature," someone or something that had put all that together.

Steve turned to face me. "Ken, do you think God is alive?" he blurted out.

I was shocked by his question. "That's crazy, Steve. I don't know. Why?"

Then he told me about several conversations he'd had with Ron, another Jewish friend. Ron believed that Jesus was the Jewish Messiah. He prayed all the time, and said he got answers from God.

"Something really strange happened after our talks and

it's got me thinking," Steve went on.

He described an experience he'd had while hitchhiking. It was very late at night, he was stranded on a lonely stretch of highway, and no one was stopping to pick him up. He was getting desperate for a ride. He saw another car coming and stuck out his thumb, but the car kept on going. He remembered Ron's challenge to him:

"Find out for yourself if God and Jesus are real. Pray, and see if you don't get an answer."

Steve was so tired he'd try anything to get a ride. As the car passed him, he prayed,

"God, I don't really believe in you, but right now I'm going to believe that if you're real, you'll get that car to stop and pick me up."

No sooner had he finished, when the car, by now about a hundred yards past him, stopped. It backed up all the way to where he was standing. The driver rolled down the window.

"Need a ride?"

Steve was shaken, amazed. "What made you come back?"

The man thought for a second. "I'm not really sure. Something just made me think I had to go back and offer you a ride."

"Ken," Steve continued, "I wonder if that was really God answering my prayer. I wonder if what Ron says about Jesus is true."

Something stirred inside me as he finished. Could it all be true? It was hard to believe, but the possibility excited me. It sure would explain a lot of things that had had me confused and wondering for so long. If there was a God, I wanted to know who He was. I felt exhilarated, and it was more than just the brisk mountain air

When I got back home, I started checking out some of the things Steve said Ron told him about Jesus and the Bible. I began looking up prophecies he had mentioned in the Old Testament that referred to Christ. When I came to the fifty-third chapter of Isaiah, I was thunderstruck as I read:

He was despised and rejected of men; a man of sorrows,

and acquainted with grief: and as one from whom men hide their face he was despised, and we esteemed him not.

Surely he hath borne our griefs inflicted by us, and suffered sorrows we have caused: yet we did esteem him stricken, smitten of God, and afflicted. But he was wounded through our transgressions, bruised through our iniquities: the chastisement of our peace was upon him, and with his wounds we were healed.

It certainly sounded like the prophet was talking about Jesus. The whole chapter seemed to fit. From all my twenty-three years of Jewish training and background, from my six years at Hebrew school, my year and a half at Hebrew College, my five years at Camp Yavneh, I had never read that portion of the Jewish Bible. Jewish training for young people doesn't stress a study of the prophetic books. I think Jewish people in general don't study the prophets because the messianic material is so controversial and hard to understand unless it is interpreted in the light of the New Testament. They usually leave those controversies to the "scholars." Still, I couldn't shake the thought as I read that this referred to Jesus. There were too many matching descriptions for it to be a coincidence.

I checked out more passages in Isaiah, and I also began to read the New Testament. I had to know the truth. At the same time I also studied many Jewish commentaries to see what our ancient sages had to say about those perplexing verses. I found that the Jewish sources didn't exactly deny the possibility of those passages referring to Messianic deliverance, but they also stated that they were not necessarily Messianic and could be interpreted otherwise. It seemed to me, however, that in order for them to come up with those other interpretations, they were bending over backwards to twist things into fitting the more acceptable explanation.

The more I read and studied, the more Jesus seemed to fit the entire picture. Could Steve and Ron be right? Was Jesus the Jewish Messiah? Halfway sincere, but still doubting even the existence of God, I began to pray, "God of Israel, if You're alive, show Yourself to me." After all, if it worked for

Steve, it could work for me, too. I began to test God. Presumptuously, I would ask Him to do small but unlikely things to prove He was really there. For example, I asked once that a certain person at my job at Beth Israel Hospital would be in a certain place, where she ordinarily wouldn't be, at a certain time, and it happened just as I asked. Looking back, I think, who was I to dare to ask for my own private little miracles? How could I demand answers from the Creator of the universe? But God was gracious and merciful, and He did answer me. Over and over again, He stooped to my weakness and showed me that He was really controlling even the smallest circumstances of my life. Even then, I wasn't sure I hadn't imagined the whole thing.

Other things were happening, too. I had enrolled in a calculus course at Boston University. The very first night of class, as I walked up to the door, I heard a passerby call out my name. It was Ron, our Jewish Christian friend. We hadn't seen each other for a long time.

"Hey, Ron, what're you doin' here?" I asked him.

"Oh, just goin' to a prayer meeting over at the student union," he answered.

I almost had a heart attack. "He's gotta be kidding!" I thought. I hadn't realized that he was so involved with this Jesus business.

It turned out he was attending a weekly Christian fellowship group led by a Jewish Christian, Mike. The group met the same time as my calculus class, and I agreed to meet Ron every week after class so we could talk. Each time I went over to see him after class, people would still be hanging around. Some of them were Jewish, and they used to talk to me about believing in Jesus. I thought that was really crazy—Jews believing in Jesus—and it made me uncomfortable when they witnessed to me all the time. Finally, Ron told them to leave me alone.

"Don't mention it to him any more," he warned. "You'll just blow him away!"

God had been trying to tell me something for a long time, but I just wasn't listening. Another time, on a camping trip with a co-worker from Beth Israel Hospital, something unusual happened. We were driving back from a really good weekend in the mountains. The way I loved camping, it had been the fulfillment of a lifelong dream, an exciting backpacking adventure in the snow. Camping was almost an idol to me, and this trip had been close to perfect. I couldn't understand why my friend and I were both depressed, coming home. Why was I so miserable after doing something I had really wanted to do for so long? This guy sitting next to me was telling me how depressed he was, too.

I thought, "What do I have to look forward to? He's older than me, and he sounds more miserable than I am. It seems that things just get worse and worse instead of better."

I started to think about humanity and all the suffering in the world. Nothing seemed to fit. There was so much strife between people, no common bond. Everyone seemed so lost. People were just floating along waiting for more misery and, ultimately, death. I was so down in spirit I cried out inside my mind, "What's the answer?"

At that very moment, a car was driving by with a bumper sticker on the back that said, "Jesus saves."

The answer was so instantaneous to my silent question that I automatically reacted with, "That's ridiculous. I'm Jewish!" Then I thought, "That didn't really happen. Somebody didn't really answer the question I was thinking." But the precision of it floored me.

Then I remembered all the things different people had been telling me about God and Jesus, and I thought, "Man, maybe they're right!" Then I thought, "No, they couldn't be right." But I couldn't put it out of my mind. I didn't want to think about it, but it was like God was chasing me. I couldn't escape it.

One morning, alone in my room, I asked God for just one more sign so I would know all the previous answers were real and not just coincidences. I felt I must resolve things in my mind once and for all because the indecision was very upsetting. I had awakened that day thinking about an old folk song I used to hear on the radio all the time. It was no longer popular and was never played any more. I picked that for the final test.

"God," I prayed, "if you really made all those other things happen, and you're really the God of Israel, then have them play that song on the radio this morning, and I'll know for sure. It doesn't have to be right now," I added magnanimously. "Any time this morning will be O.K., and I'll know it's from you." I still can't believe that I actually had the gall to give Him a two-hour deadline!

Even while I prayed, in a way I hoped He wouldn't answer. Then I could go back to my "normal" state of affairs and not have to deal with the conflicts my budding faith had raised. If I had just imagined the whole thing, everything would be so much easier. Then I could forget all this nonsense and start living my life in what I hoped would be a more mature fashion. Still, on the other hand, part of me hoped that He was real, and I was excited about the prospect of finding out the truth, at last.

As soon as I finished praying, I walked out of my room. Just as I passed my sister's room down the hall, I heard her radio playing the very song I had asked for. A shock went through my body like lightning. I found myself shaking from the emotional impact, yet very joyful.

"Wow!" I thought. "This is nothing to fool around with!" I was so excited, I felt like jumping up and down. I wanted to run out in the street and yell, "Hey, everyone, God is real! He's real!" But I knew I couldn't do that. People would think I had lost my mind.

I had been afraid to know the truth. Now I wasn't afraid any more. I knew God had met me in a very special way, and no one could ever take that knowledge from me. I felt like maybe God was standing there smiling at me indulgently, saying "Well, here I am, Ken, what are you going to do about it?" Then, for a while, it was like a new game to me. For two weeks I kept asking God for other signs, even though I had promised Him I wouldn't ask for any more. He rebuked me with silence. Finally I realized that He had taken me at my word when I asked for "just one more sign" with that song, and I dared not ask for more.

About this time I came under heavy conviction. I realized that I was a sinner and that things weren't yet right between me and God.

I told Steve what had happened to me because I knew he'd understand. He told me, "Now that God has revealed Himself to you, He expects you to act on your faith. You must make a commitment to Him. Accept Jesus into your life."

I fought that idea for about three more weeks, but God wouldn't let me rest. I couldn't stop thinking about it.

"O.K., Jesus," I prayed, "if you're really alive, I'll give my life to you." I was still holding back a little by qualifying my prayer with that "if."

Three more days passed. I was miserable with the constant knowledge that I had unfinished business with God. It weighed on me heavily, until I could no longer ignore it. I told Steve, "I'm ready to give my life to Jesus."

Steve was happy for me, but uncertain. "I'm so new at all this myself," he said. "I'd better call Ron. He'll know what to do." We went to Ron's house, and there he helped me pray the sinner's prayer of confession, faith, and commitment to Christ. I became a new person in Jesus that evening, and I was amazed at the strange new happiness and peace that filled me.

That night at Ron's house, Artie and Al, my future roommates, were there. I never imagined then that I'd end up living with them.

After I made my decision to follow Jesus, I became more friendly with Ron because he was sort of following me up. He called me the next day after I accepted the Lord and asked how I was doing and invited me to go the next Wednesday to a prayer meeting at a place called the Cenacle. The people there were all "born-again" Catholics, and Ron was the "token Jew."

In addition to the Cenacle, Ron was affiliated with Jews for Jesus. Periodically he'd been going out on the streets with them, witnessing and handing out literature.

"Boy," I told him, "you'll never catch me doing that, going out on the streets."

I especially wasn't sure about Jews for Jesus. I didn't know who or what they were. I hadn't really ever heard of them before. Ron told me they were just beginning to be active in Boston and I might enjoy meeting some of them. I figured I'd go over there sometime because I was Jewish and I believed in Jesus. Besides, I wanted to check them out.

During this time, Ron called me whenever he could, but we really didn't have a chance to see one another much. I had just left my job at the hospital and was taking some time off before starting school again. My first answer to prayer as a new believer was getting accepted at school. I had tried before without success. Bored with my job, I knew I shouldn't just quit without having a definite goal in mind. I realized it wasn't right just to stagnate. Now God had given me my answer. I could go back to school, and I was excited about that. I took a short vacation first, and when I came back, my sister told me that someone had called and left a message while I was gone. That someone was Mike, who led the Bible study. He told me that the New Jerusalem Players, a Jews for Jesus drama group, was going to be at Ruggles Street Baptist Church the next Sunday, and I ought to go see them. I went down to the church and watched them present a "Christ in the Passover" program. This was the first I ever really saw of Jews for Jesus. About a month later, Ron told me Jews for Jesus was having a meeting to see who wanted to start a Bible study at someone's house, and it was by invitation only. Then he called back and said it was O.K. that I come.

I went to that meeting and heard Jeff Fritz, the leader, explain about the Jews for Jesus ministry, what was going on, and what they planned for the future. I met many other Jewish believers there. I was surprised; I didn't realize there were so many. At that point, I started going to the Jews for Jesus Bible studies, and have continued ever since.

Jeff started a study about the messiahship of Jesus. Was He, or was He not the Messiah? We started going over Messianic prophecies from the beginning. I recognized many of them that I already knew, and there were some new ones I hadn't seen before. I knew believing in Jesus was right. It all seemed to fit. Still, I had more than just prophecies on which

I based my faith. I had the experience of answered prayer.

So many things happened to me that first year I came to Christ. I couldn't believe them all. They were blowing my mind, there were so many instances of God showing me He was there and He cared. One night, I was spared from three separate car accidents, three really heavy things that showed me God was there all the time, whether I knew it or not.

I really enjoyed the Jews for Jesus Bible studies. I looked forward to them every week, and many times I stayed late. Because Jeff knew I was a new believer, many times he'd tell me to stick around afterwards and we'd go over Scriptures together. I'd ask questions, and we'd have almost a second Bible study and fellowship, just the two of us. Sometimes I felt guilty about taking so much of his time. Often Joanna, his wife, would get tired and go upstairs. It'd be midnight, and Jeff would be getting sleepy before I was ready to leave. Once he told me, "I enjoy this, so don't worry about putting me out."

During my second semester of school, Jeff arranged to have personal Bible studies with me on a separate day from the regular Bible study so we'd have more time. He knew I was under a lot of pressure at home and the extra study would help me. I started going to his house some mornings during school vacation for Bible study, and we got into the book of I John. We went over the whole book, and I got a lot out of it. I'd spend just about the whole day there, from morning through lunch, and into the afternoon.

Sometimes if I was free, I'd go and hand out literature with Joanna Fritz and Dave Brickner, another Jewish Christian who was living at Jeff's house. At first I was nervous about doing that, but then I got so I enjoyed it. A large part of my reticence was due to not wanting to embarrass my parents. I knew there was always the possibility of meeting people who knew my parents while I was out witnessing on the streets. I didn't go out until after I was no longer living at home. During September and October, I was still living at home, but by mid-October, things were so strained that I finally moved out about the first of November.

Chapter 4

Now I See It—Now You Don't

> I will praise thee, O LORD, among the people: and I will
> sing praises unto thee among the nations. For thy mercy is
> great above the heavens: and thy truth reacheth unto the
> clouds. (Psalm 108:3, 4)

Can you shut off a fast mountain stream? Can anyone
hold back the incoming ocean tides? Nor can anyone make
a new Christian keep quiet about his faith in Christ. My happiness and excitement about my new relationship with the
God of Israel grew until I couldn't contain it. I just had to tell
people. Even before I decided to quit and go back to school,
my co-workers at Beth Israel Hospital had noticed the
change in me. I was much happier and had become more
optimistic, and everyone noticed.

I tried to show my parents some prophecies from Isaiah
and Micah that had impressed me so much the first time I
read them. In the beginning they were willing to talk, even
were happy and impressed that I wanted to read the Bible.
But soon they began to resist when they realized I was interested in Jesus. The only way my father ever wanted to discuss the matter of Jesus was to show me articles or books he
found that denied any possibility of Jesus being the Messiah.
I wanted him to read the New Testament so we could discuss
matters intelligently, but he wouldn't. He only wanted to convince me of his viewpoint without listening to mine.

My mother reacted with anger, bitterness, and fear. She
had even more of a problem with my new theology than my
father because she held an important position in the Jewish
community, teaching fifth grade children at a Boston Hebrew school. She absolutely dreaded anyone finding out that
her son was even thinking about Jesus.

By this time I was attending regular Bible studies, and it
dawned on my parents that I believed more about Jesus than
they could comfortably accept, even if I kept quiet about it. I
hadn't actually told them about the full commitment I had

made, and one day they confronted me.

"What does all this mean? We're afraid you're going to become a Christian."

I told them I already was a Christian, that I had committed my life to God through Christ. Their anger bordered on hysteria. At times my mother would look at me with wild fear in her eyes.

"Don't tell anybody your crazy ideas!" she'd scream at me. "I'll lose my job on account of you!"

This all happened at the Jewish New Year season, in September of 1976. After that time, whenever I left the house to attend the weekly Bible studies, my parents yelled and made a scene. They evidently thought if they made a big enough fuss about it, I wouldn't go. But they were mistaken. I needed the fellowship of other believers, and the spiritual nourishment I was getting. It was worth the pain and aggravation I suffered each time I went through one of those scenes.

One night my parents arranged for me to see an orthodox Lubavitch rabbi. For their sake, I agreed to go, even though I knew he wouldn't dissuade me. It was only about a week after they found out about my decision, and they were very upset about my being involved with Jews for Jesus. They thought it was some weird cult, and I had been brainwashed by them.

Before my appointment with the rabbi, my parents overheard me on the telephone, telling Jeff Fritz that I was going. My father said he knew the Jews for Jesus people were just waiting to get their hands on me the minute I came back from the rabbi. Evidently my parents didn't think I had much of a mind of my own. They figured the rabbi could talk me out of the "nonsense" I was espousing, and then Jews for Jesus would brainwash me right back into it. Because I had had a difficult time maturing during my adolescence, they gave me no credit now for being able to think seriously or make valid decisions. They refused to see that at last I had grown up and gained purpose and stability. They particularly couldn't admit this to themselves because to their way of thinking—any Jew who believed in Jesus couldn't be in his right mind.

Obediently, to show respect, I went to the rabbi's house for an evening of discussion. As we conversed, he seemed not to know exactly what was going on with me.

"What are you doing here?" he asked. "Your mother called me on the telephone, practically hysterical, asking that I talk to you because you believe in Jesus."

He thought I believed because I had emotional problems, that something was missing in my life, and that I was searching in the wrong place for fulfillment.

"Judaism could fill that need just as well," he counselled me. "You should go to a yeshivah and study Jewish things. You aren't qualified to make this kind of decision without doing a great deal of study."

I told him I had already studied quite a bit in Hebrew school, and I brought up passages from the prophets that I felt were Messianic. He had his own answers for every Messianic passage to prove that it didn't refer to Jesus. Finally, he became agitated and said the only thing that ever came of Christianity was bloodshed.

"Why do you believe this?" he asked.

I countered his question with some of my own. "The God of Israel," I asked, "does He still speak as He spoke to His prophets? Is there a way to reach Him? Does He still communicate with us as He did back in Bible days? I want to know. Where is the God of Israel?"

The rabbi looked at me and didn't say anything. I could tell he was shaken by my questions and didn't have an answer. After a long pause, he said, "Well, we'll come to that. I'll speak to you about that later."

I knew right then that he didn't know, that he had no answers. He tried to discuss with me the importance of the Jewish ritual. I told him that to me ritual meant nothing without the heart behind it. He tried to convince me that sometimes it's good just to do a thing because it's right, rather than for a good motive. He said the ritual gave meaning to his life.

After that lecture, he finished with, "So! I live empty religion. That's what I do."

I couldn't believe he said that. I left with mixed feelings, rather confused. I thought, if Jesus isn't the Messiah, then there's no God at all! Still, I felt that God was real, because He had answered my prayers. The rabbi couldn't kill that spark of faith in me even though he had succeeded in confusing me.

When I came home from seeing the rabbi, I called Jeff. "How do you feel about things?" he asked.

I told him I was confused, and he invited me to talk to him the next day. I had dinner with him at his house, and we discussed many Scripture passages. When my parents heard about that, they were furious.

"Of course!" they fumed. "Jeff got you right away and brainwashed you back into it."

My mother kept after me to go to the rabbi again, but I really didn't want to, and I kept putting it off. The next week, as I was walking down the street to go to the weekly Bible study at Jeff's house, I found myself surrounded by about ten bearded orthodox Jewish students.

When I first saw them farther down the block, I had a feeling they were waiting for me. I thought, "Oh no! What should I do?" Then I figured maybe God wanted me to witness to them, so I walked right into it.

One of them came up to me and asked, "Are you Jewish?"

I wanted to see what they were up to. "What difference does that make? What're you doing here?"

"Well, we're just looking for Jewish people," he said. That was ridiculous, because Jeff's house is in a very Irish Catholic neighborhood. It was obvious that they had a specific plan, and it probably directly involved me.

They coaxed and badgered me into going with them in a car to another orthodox rabbi's house. It was during the Feast of Booths (Tabernacles), and we sat and talked in a *succah*, which is a booth especially constructed for that holiday.

We sat for a long time, discussing God, miracles, and Chasidism, the strict Jewish sect to which these people belonged. It was getting late, and they were making me miss the Bible study. I kept telling them I wanted to go, and they kept talking so I couldn't leave, telling me stories about their rabbi, who sounded to me like a Jewish guru. They thought this rabbi had miraculous powers and insights.

I kept insisting that I wanted to leave. Finally they took me back to Jeff's house, but not until after the Bible study was over. I wanted to talk to Jeff about it, but it was so late that the lights were out already, and I didn't want to disturb him. When I spoke to him about it the next day, he said those people had approached his house before I got there, probably looking for me. When I accused my mother of putting them up to it, she vigorously denied it. I backed off, really not sure whether she had done it or not. She sounded so convincing at the time.

By November, life at home was intolerable. I had planned to stay at my parents' home for another semester for convenience's sake, but now I knew I had to get a place of my own. My friend Steve and I found a comfortable house for rent in a nice neighborhood. It was a quiet location, with trees, and the rent was cheap. We both felt it was an answer to prayer. Maybe it was cheap and quiet because it was near a cemetery, but we didn't care about that. As a Christian, I could now face the concept of death without fear. If the cemetery location made the house cheaper, that was fine with me.

Unfortunately, not long after we took the house together, Steve began to doubt the messiahship of Jesus. My parents found out about that and kept pressuring him to get me to change my mind, too. We had some heavy discussions about religion from time to time, but finally Steve told my parents he wasn't going to pester me about my faith anymore. He could see that I was a different, much happier person because of it, so why should he try to change me? Still, he used to argue with me about my going to the Jews for Jesus Bible studies. But I liked the Bible studies. It was comforting and reassuring to know that many others of my fellow Jews also believed in Jesus. I also started attending St. Paul's Evangelical Church in Somerville, Massachusetts, on a regular basis. My faith grew and held firm, despite the fact that my parents had now hit on a new plan to dissuade me from my beliefs.

One day I received a letter from a Steve Jacobs, whom I had never met. He wrote, "Your mother told me you are interested in the Bible, and I'd like to discuss the issue with you." In subsequent letters and lengthy two-hour long distance telephone calls from Philadelphia, he kept bringing up arguments to persuade me that Jesus was not the Messiah and that I could believe in God without Him. He also tried laying "guilt trips" on me about how badly I was treating my parents by believing in Jesus. I knew he was hired by my parents because sometimes he would send me copies of letters he had written them outlining what he had discussed with me over the telephone and the progress he thought he made. Those long distance phone calls must have cost my parents a bundle. It's really sad that they felt they had to do that.

In the meantime, I had met Christine early in 1977 at a Jews for Jesus monthly social. Even though she was a Gentile believer, she enjoyed the Jewish flavor of the Bible studies and meetings. They gave her insights into the Jewish roots of her faith. Though I found her attractive, I struggled with my feelings for several months, because of my childhood conditioning against Jews intermarrying with Gentiles, wondering how my parents would react if anything serious developed between Chris and me. Finally I came to the conclusion that Jesus had lived and died just to break down such false barriers, and I felt free to date her seriously. Not long after that decision, we fell in love. We sought God's will in the matter, and felt we had His blessing on our marriage plans. I had told my parents in October, 1977, that I was seeing Chris and they refused to deal with it. When in January, 1978, I told them of our engagement, the roof fell in. First I had become a Christian—to them, it was the same as rejecting my own people—now I was marrying a Gentile. Their anger and accusations knew no bounds. They devised a fantastic idea that I didn't really want to marry Christine. I was a weak person, easily led by others, and Christine, in cahoots with Jews for Jesus, had manipulated me into the whole situation. My mother began a campaign to stop the marriage.

On several occasions Christine received phone calls from my mother, describing me as immature, incompetent, and a totally worthless person. As another tactic, she tried to pressure Christine into converting to Judaism. When all these attempts failed, she promised to stop the wedding at all costs.

"We have ways of breaking things up," my parents warned on one occasion.

"Don't try anything illegal," I cautioned them. "You'd only get yourselves in trouble. Why don't you just try to accept things as they are." I didn't really think, though, that they would stoop to such extremes as abduction or physical harm to either of us.

Nevertheless, as the wedding date drew closer and my parents continued to threaten, we felt we ought to have an alternate plan. The wedding was officially scheduled for Sunday, May 21st. We planned our rehearsal for the previous Thursday. At that rehearsal, we were going through the entire ceremony, vows and all. If, somehow, my parents found a way to stop or ruin the ceremony on Sunday, our pastor would simply date the wedding certificate as of Thursday. Our pastor agreed to this plan. If at first he hadn't thought that my family was capable of causing such a disruption, he changed his mind when a couple of weeks before the scheduled date he had a strange phone call late one night. Claiming to represent the Jewish Defense League, a militant Jewish group, the caller identified himself and in a rude and threatening voice mocked, "I understand that you're planning a wedding this month."

Even then, we couldn't really foresee the testings and hardships that lay ahead of us—not until that Thursday night in Newton.

Chapter 5
Acts Revisited

Be merciful unto me, O God, be merciful unto me: for my soul trusteth in thee: yea, in the shadow of thy wings will I make my refuge, until these calamities be overpast.

I will cry unto God most high; unto God that performeth all things for me.

He shall send from heaven, and save me from the reproach of him that would swallow me up. Selah. God shall send forth his mercy and his truth.

My soul is among lions: and I lie even among them that are set on fire, even the sons of men, whose teeth are spears and arrows, and their tongue a sharp sword.

Be thou exalted, O God above the heavens; let thy glory be above all the earth. (Psalm 57:1-5)

As I bumped along in the kidnap van with my abductors, I tried to assess my situation. I couldn't afford to panic. The fear that had first gripped me when they seized me gave way to anger. How dare they do this? Surely it must be illegal. Then slowly my anger was replaced by feelings of excitement. Though I was beginning to feel bruises all over my body from the struggle, and I was lying in a very uncomfortable position with my hands and feet tied, and two fellows were literally sitting on me, I started to feel agitated but still strangely happy. I was being allowed to suffer for my faith! The problem went deeper than my parents' resentment at my marrying Christine, a non-Jew. They were convinced that my faith in Christ was irrational, and that the friends I had made at the Jews for Jesus Bible studies had some sort of weird hold on me. At one point, even before I told them about Chris, they had threatened to have me deprogrammed. Now, here I was bound, bruised, and being taken I didn't know where by a group of people who obviously had been hired by my parents to dissuade me not only from my marriage, but from my faith in Jesus.

I prayed, thanking God for being entrusted with suffering for His sake. I'm generally not the martyr type, and never would have asked for such a situation. Still, now that I was in the middle of it, what a fantastic opportunity to see God work things out! I praised Him, certain that He would soon rescue me. I knew that Jesus was real, I knew that my faith was real, and Christine and I both felt that it was God's will for us to marry. With all this in my favor, God wouldn't let my abductors get away with this. He would soon work some kind of miracle, I thought, to get me out of this predicament. Maybe the van would have a flat tire, or engine trouble, and the highway patrol would come. I was sure something would happen. Uncomfortable, but not too concerned for the moment, I was eager and excited to see how God would manifest His power and control.

While I was thinking these thoughts, I felt the van slow down. We must have travelled at least fifteen minutes at a fairly high speed on what felt like a major highway. Now we stopped. I heard both side doors being opened and the two fellows who were sitting on me got off. They couldn't agree on how to get me out of the van. One pushed and one pulled, and they almost dropped me, head down. Finally they go me out and carried me, lengthwise, into a building. It must have been some kind of enclosed courtyard or garden area, because they weren't trying to hide me from view. What would the neighbors think if they saw us, I wondered. Would they chalk it up to some sort of fraternity stunt? It was the wrong time of year for that. Would they call the police?

Once inside the building, I could feel they were carrying me up a steep staircase with several turns in it. At the top of the stairs, they opened the door of a room and dumped me on a bed. At that point, I was afraid they were going to give me a shot to knock me out. I struggled and fought to get free. Someone jabbed his knee into the small of my back and grabbed me under the chin.

"You'd better not move, or you'll get yourself killed," he

threatened. "We'll break your head. We're not kidding! If you keep quiet and listen to us, everything will be all right. Just relax."

I think my father left right after they brought me upstairs. I heard his voice for a minute, as though he had just stuck his head in the room to check it out. Then I didn't hear his voice anymore. When I asked later where he was, someone said, "He left a long time ago."

As I sat on the bed in the upstairs room they untied me and took off the hood, and for the first time I saw my captors. I looked around. They had me in an attic room with a steeply pitched ceiling and boarded up windows. There were three people in the room. One was a short, heavy fellow in his late teens or early twenties. Dressed in a pullover shirt and casual type pants, he wore a black yarmulke on his head like an orthodox Jew, but his brown hair was short, and he had no beard. He puffed nervously at a cigarette.

"See how your father loves you." He pointed at an air conditioner in the room. "He wanted to make sure you'd be comfortable."

I recognized his voice. He was the one who had threatened to break my head in the van, and who had sat on me.

The second fellow I noticed was the one whose hand I had bitten. He, too, was heavy, more muscular than fat, and tall. His curly black hair frizzed out long and full, almost to his shoulders and covered his cheeks and chin. Whoever the rest of these people were, they had chosen well for the abduction, I thought. Both of these guys were really big bruisers.

I looked at the second fellow who was standing near the door. "Sorry I bit you," I offered.

"S'awright," he shrugged. Then he left.

The third fellow, Kalman, looked about twenty-four. He was about five feet eight or so. His dark beard was sparse and scraggly, as though he had been trying to grow it for a while without too much success. Another heavyweight, this one also wore a black yarmulke on the back of his head.

"Do you want to get up and walk around?" someone asked.

I got up and headed for the window side of the room. By now it must have been about 7:30 in the evening. Dusky light was still coming in through some chinks in the boarded up windows. I saw a slit on one side large enough to see through, and caught a quick glimpse of a steep roof line, reddish frame building and some sort of flowering fruit tree in the yard. The house seemed to be sitting at the top of a hill on a busy street with two-way traffic.

"Don't look out!" someone ordered. I walked away from the window. Shocked, dazed, I was beginning to realize that I was not going to make that wedding rehearsal. I felt terrible that Christine and our friends would worry when I didn't show up.

They were still trying to impress me that my parents were doing this because they loved me. I wasn't buying that. Angry and frustrated, I leaned back in my chair to a window behind me and tore off one of the boards that was only taped on. I flung it across the room at one of the kidnappers. It narrowly missed him, just grazing his arm. At this, the two jumped on me and tied me up again.

"If you act like an animal, we'll treat you like an animal," one threatened.

I still had some fight left in me. "If you treat me like a human being, I'll act human!"

Now a series of people began coming into the room, one or two at a time. They all looked young, in their twenties, and wore the garb of orthodox Jews—skull cap or wide-brimmed black hat, and fringed undergarments that showed at the bottoms of their shirts. They untied my hands again and bombarded me with questions.

They found out my Hebrew name was Chayim and used that instead of "Ken." I figured that was step number one in their trying to impress me with my Jewish heritage, so I would give up my faith in Jesus. Of course, they didn't realize that to my way of thinking, one had nothing to do with the other. That is, I felt then and still do feel perfectly comfortable maintaining my Jewish ethnic heritage while believing in Jesus as my Messiah, Lord, and Savior.

In demanding tones they asked—Who was I? What did I

believe? They kept insisting that Jesus wasn't the Messiah and tried to persuade me with Scriptures that Christianity wasn't true.

"Why would God become a man? What a stupid thing for Him to do!" they taunted.

They intimated that it wasn't intelligent for anyone to believe such things. They read passages from the New Testament and said they were full of contradictions and couldn't be the Word of God.

All night people kept coming in and leaving. They wouldn't let me sleep or think. I tried to close my eyes and pray instead of answering their questions. When I did this, they yelled, "You'll never get out of here if you don't talk!" Every time I started to doze off, they either violently shook me awake and screamed at me to sit up straight, or Kalman, the one with the scraggly beard, slammed a yardstick down about two inches from my face. Finally they made me stand up so I wouldn't go to sleep. When I fell asleep on my feet, they made me walk, held up between two of them.

Then they began to accuse me of being an anti-Semite.

"What you believe breeds anti-Semitism! Christians are responsible for the Holocaust in Germany. Anyone that embraces Christianity is a Jew hater and has no feelings. You Nazi! How does it feel to be locked up in an attic like Ann Frank?"

They made me read New Tesament passages out loud and then ridiculed them.

"Where is your God now?" they taunted. "Why doesn't He rescue you if He's so powerful?"

Just a few days before this I had been meditating on Jesus' sufferings. Now I thought of Him enduring similar taunts as He hung on the cross, and I felt a special kinship with Him. I snatched brief seconds of silent prayer, still believing that God would rescue me when the time was right.

Whenever I asked about my family or my father, or Christine, they responded "Your family and friends know all about this." On one occasion, one person told me, "Your father has had it with you, Chayim; he's forgotten you."

"Look," I pleaded, "I'm supposed to be some place. They'll worry."

"Forget it, you're not going anywhere." They had taken away my belt and sneakers so I couldn't run away too easily.

"Well, then," I begged, "just let me make a telephone call."

They refused. Several times I tried to escape. I'd jump up, hit the light switch, and make for the door. Each time they overpowered me. I found out later I had a broken nose, probably from one of these episodes.

The harassment and sleeplessness continued into the next day. They offered me some food, but I refused. I was too upset by then to eat. They took me, blindfolded and guarded, to the bathroom when necessary.

I approached one who seemed more sympathetic than the rest. His name was Pinchas.

"When can I leave?"

His answer frightened me. "When you're out of the wash. One fellow was here for six months. You'd better get used to this place!"

Chapter 6
Darkness in Daylight

The second day of my captivity in the Boston attic, five people came in, carrying about ten cardboard boxes, heavy duty tape, scissors, razors, knives, and hammers. The room was filled with them and with the sounds of hammering and ripping cardboard. They started taping layers and layers of cardboard over the already boarded up windows, joking all the while. I lay on the bed and watched, amazed that they would go to so much trouble.

"Boy," one laughed. "It's going to be so dark in here with the lights off that we'll be able to develop pictures."

After that the only way I could tell if it was night or day was by the chirping of birds outside, or by the increase and decrease of traffic noises on the road below the house.

New people kept coming up in shifts to relieve those who grew tired, and the badgering and questioning continued. I was trying hard to hang onto the thought that God soon would rescue me. I thought of all the Bible accounts I had read about miraculous rescues . . . the angel opening the door of Peter's prison in the Book of Acts, the Old Testament story of Jehovah making a deep sleep fall over Israel's enemies before a battle. Maybe my jailers would all fall asleep and I'd just walk out. Maybe the police would come. Maybe . . .

Then on Saturday something strange did happen. Suddenly, amid all the questioning and harassment, all the lights went out. My stomach jumped with the thought, "Maybe this is it!" There was scuffling and momentary confusion, and I heard someone say sarcastically, "Could this be an act of God?"

My hopes were dashed when they found it was only a blown fuse from the overworked air conditioner. They fixed it fast, and the lights went back on. When those lights went on, it was like a light inside *me* went off. Frustrated, fatigued beyond description, lightheaded from not eating, I began to sink into despair. Looking back now, I wonder if that power failure might not have been God's unheeded warning to my persecutors:

"Ken is my child through faith in Christ. Let him go!" If it was God's message, they, like so many of my people, were blind and deaf to it. Still, maybe some day one of my captors will remember that attic scene and be drawn to consider Christ because of it.

After they untied me, at least I could move around a little. Sometimes I got so nervous I paced up and down very agitatedly. I kept asking what day it was.

"Why are you so upset?" they'd respond. "What's the big hurry? Where do you have to go?" They wouldn't tell me what day it was.

"I'm supposed to get married. I have to get out!" I pleaded.

They looked at me knowingly. "Married? You were going to get married? But the girl isn't Jewish. You couldn't have gotten married. It's against Jewish law, a sin! Your marriage wouldn't have lasted. Your children wouldn't be Jewish, and you'd be unhappy and end up getting a divorce."

For three days this kind of questioning, taunting, and sleeplessness went on. Some time on the second day, I said I was hungry, and they brought me an orange. Later they brought another orange and a piece of cold chicken.

By the the end of the third day the harassment had grown even uglier. A big, red-haired guy, Shmuel, was one of my chief tormentors. He made me stand with a New Testament balanced on my head and screamed at me, just inches away from my face so I would recoil and make the book fall. My face was wet with his saliva. Then he made me pick the book up and do it again, saying, "You're going to be in big trouble if you let it fall again." Orthodox Jews have a superstition about dropping a holy book. They regard it as a sin and immediately kiss the book on both covers as an act of devotion and contrition. I guess they thought I would feel guilty about letting the Bible fall. They did that and everything they could think of to wear me down by waging a war of nerves against me.

Then they decided to wear me down further with physical exhaustion. They turned off the air conditioner, and the attic quickly became unbearably hot. They made me stand motionless, at attention, for a long time. My shirt stuck to my back in big patches of sweat and I felt weak, dizzy, and depressed. I found myself beginning to doubt that God would ever rescue me. The kidnappers were sweating, too, in that close, sweltering heat, but they wouldn't turn the air conditioning back on.

Shmuel looked at me with hatred. "It's worth being uncomfortable just to see you suffer, you Nazi!" he sneered. "Let's see you do ten pushups!"

I was afraid of him, and I wearily complied.

"Very good," he drawled. He turned to the short, fat fellow, one of the original kidnappers, who was in the room with us. "Why don't you do some?"

"Naw, I don't want to."

"Go ahead, do 'em," Shmuel insisted.

The little guy obeyed and laboriously did ten pushups.

"Now both of you do them together," Shmuel instructed. "I'll count."

"No," I protested. "I'm too tired."

Shmuel glared at me. "DO 'EM!"

I didn't dare refuse. The little guy and I did thirty pushups altogether. Maybe he was afraid of Shmuel, too. Shmuel could intimidate anyone. During the questioning and harassment, he would narrow his eyes at me and spit out through clenched teeth, "I hate you! People like you do not deserve to live!" Then he'd abruptly change his manner and say in carefully measured tones, "Don't make me lose my temper. I've lost my temper before." He'd turn away and punch the wall for effect, or pick up a New Testament and throw it across the room. His alternate manner of restraint and almost maniacal behavior produced a blood-chilling effect on me. I was thankful now that he hadn't insisted on more pushups.

By that time I figured as closely as I could that it was probably Sunday, the evening of my wedding day, and past the time when the ceremony would have taken place. This added to my discouragement. All along I had been clinging to the hope that surely God would get me out of there in time for the wedding. Now I realized that He wasn't going to. Lack of food, lack of sleep, physical and emotional exhaustion, began to take their toll. I knew I'd have to negotiate with my captors or they'd never let me go.

"O.K.," I panted, "what do you want me to do?"

"Swear that you'll never tell another Jewish person about Jesus!"

I shook my head. "I can't do that."

"Well, then, we'll keep you here."

They continued their little war of nerves until I thought I couldn't stand it another minute. Again I asked, "What do you want from me?"

"Denounce Jesus! Say he's burning in hell, and we'll let you go."

A wave of nausea swept from the pit of my stomach to my throat. I clenched my teeth until my jaws ached and said nothing. When they saw that I wouldn't blaspheme Jesus, they started screaming at me, harassing again, shouting abuse. This lasted again for hours. One person kept trying to get me to say, "Jesus isn't the Messiah; the New Testament isn't real." The more I protested that I couldn't say that in good conscience, the more he kept screaming at me, "Say it!" It was getting very late, and I fell asleep under that treatment, sitting in a chair. I must have dozed for only a moment. Then he was standing over me, shaking me, looking happy, as if he had finally accomplished someting.

"There! You said it as you were falling asleep."

I stared at him groggily. "I don't remember saying it. I didn't mean to say it!"

"Oh, you said it all right!"

I didn't think I really had, but I couldn't be sure. I was so sleepy. I thought I'd better try to lead them on and negotiate again. By now a more sympathetic fellow was in charge of the new shift. It was the same one, Pinchas. He'd been with me from the time I was first brought to the attic, and I felt I could relate to him better than the others. He was less violent.

"Look, Pinchas," I told him, "I can agree that you have reasons not to believe in Jesus that seem valid to you. I can see things from your point of view. Let me go now, and I'll study these matters and check out what you're saying. But you know you can't force me to change my mind so fast. I need to investigate some more for myself."

He promised that he would speak to someone about letting me go, and left. Soon a couple of the others came back upstairs.

"You're lying," Kalman accused. "You're not really interested in studying Judaism. Would you really commit yourself to going to Israel to a Jewish school for at least a year? I don't think you're sincere. God just gave me a special revelation. He told me you're lying, and He said He doesn't wanna have nuthin' to do with you. You're not only an anti-Semite, you're a liar, too!"

While this was going on I heard scuffling and voices outside the attic room. People were gathering around the door, trying to listen. The door was ajar. I got up and looked and saw that they had a tape recorder and were waiting for me to make some big pronouncement of unbelief. I sensed as some of them came into the room that something was about to happen, because they looked happier than before.

The kidnappers brought up a large unleavened wafer and some beer. After the matzo wafer, I was so desperately thirsty I downed the beer like a dying man in the desert. I found out later they had deliberately given me alcohol on an almost empty stomach so I would sleep when they moved me. Also, they figured it would make me feel guilty.

A little while later they took me on one of my guarded bathroom trips. As usual, two people went with me. One stayed outside the door, and the other stood in the shower to give me some semblance of privacy. They wouldn't leave me alone in there because there was a window I might climb through. While I was in the bathroom, I heard voices arguing and negotiating outside. As I left the bathroom, the short, fat fellow, the one who had done pushups with me, came over. He patted me on the back, a gesture very much out of character with his previous behavior toward me.

"Well, Chayim, I'm not gonna see you anymore. I wantcha to take it easy. Nice knowin' ya. Good luck, and I hope everything works out O.K. for you. Just take it easy. Remember, do what they say and you'll be all right."

Then someone else said "O.K., Chayim, we're gonna move you now. We're taking you to the Boss." He gave me back my shoes.

"Oh, good," I thought. "Maybe they'll let me go soon."

As they were getting me ready, red-haired Shmuel, the wall puncher, approached me menacingly.

"If you try anything, you're gonna be very sorry. Don't fool around if you know what's good for you. You might fool the others, but you'll never fool me!"

I was more afraid of that one than any of the others. I decided I'd better do as he said. I went quickly. They blindfolded me again, but left my feet free to walk out of the house. As the cool evening breeze hit my face, I held back for a second. It felt so good to take a deep breath of fresh air. They hurried me into the back seat of a car and made me lie down. A guard sat by each door. One had my head on his lap. I think it was Pinchas, the milder mannered one. Another had my feet, and they covered me from sight with a blanket.

"We're going for a nice long ride now, and you'll be able to sleep," they told me.

"What kind of a ride?" I wondered. Surely they weren't planning to kill me!

It was stuffy and dark under the blanket, and I was so exhausted I fell asleep almost immediately. It wasn't a deep sleep, though. I alternately dozed and woke and sensed that we were going through toll booths on a major highway. Every so often the car slowed down and they'd tug at the blanket to make sure I was all covered and warn me not to move around. Then I'd hear whispered discussions and directions, like "No, no, take that one," or "Over there! Over there!" or "Be careful! Watch out!" Then I'd heard the clink of coins. I thought they must be avoiding car lineups and manned toll booths because they were afraid of being seen.

I found out later that they had been really worried taking me in the car like that. They knew what they were doing was illegal, and whenever they saw police cars they were afraid.

It seemed we crossed some bridges because I thought I smelled salt water. We traveled for a long, long time, and I thought we were probably going south from the Boston area. There are many toll booths in that area, going down to New York and New Jersey.

After what must have been many hours, the car finally stopped. The lack of motion must have awakened me. I felt stiff all over, but somewhat more rested than I had been for a very long time. Through my blindfold I sensed daylight. I heard rain on the car roof and voices arguing. What were they going to do now?

Chapter 7
Give It Up, Already

I heard the kidnappers arguing about how to get me from the car without being seen. They didn't want to take off my blindfold. Still, if anyone saw me wearing it, they might wonder what was going on. Finally they decided to take me out blindfolded with the blanket over me. That wouldn't look too strange, since it was raining. They led me out by the hand, steering me into a house and down some stairs. After walking me in circles several times, they removed the blindfold.

They had me in a basement room with no windows and only one door. The walls were white. The only furnishings consisted of a low, narrow cot, three large work tables, and a high swivel stool with a padded vinyl seat. Two of the tables were set up with equipment for rewinding 16mm movie reels. I sat on the third table with my legs dangling down. They left me there with Pinchas, who kept trying to persuade me to give in.

"Give it up, Chayim, give it up already." He looked tired.

"Give what up?" I asked innocently.

"The belief!"

"How can I give it up? I believe it's true."

"You'll be here an awfully long time if you don't," he warned.

I couldn't seem to make him understand that I couldn't stop believing just because someone told me I must. We talked for almost two hours about the doctrinal differences between Christianity and Judaism. Then other people started coming in. They were mostly new faces I hadn't seen in the Boston attic.

Three young men came in together. They looked like students to me, in their early twenties, all with beards and head coverings like the very orthodox Jews. I thought they might be yeshivah students from a nearby Jewish school.

They seemed to be waiting around to see what would happen next. Then more people came in. One was a tall, heavy man about forty years old. Another was a plump, pleasant faced thirtyish looking young woman. I could tell that her elaborate hairdo was a wig, such as those worn by very orthodox Jewish women who only appear bareheaded before their own husbands. Her clothing, also in the modest orthodox tradition, covered her to the elbows and halfway to her ankles.

"Hullo," she greeted me. "Are you hungry?" Would you like something to eat?"

"Yeah, I would." I smiled gratefully. I was really glad to see her. I figured maybe with a woman in the group, these new people would be less violent. Boy, was I wrong!

As she left to get the food, another tall, heavy man came into the basement room. He, too, was wearing a yarmulke, the Jewish skull cap, and he carried a Bible. He stormed over to where I was sitting on the table and gestured with his Bible in my face.

"So you believe in Jesus, huh?" He turned to the others. "Wanta get a sword for him? Go upstairs, someone, and get a sword!" He turned back to me. "I want you to slay me with the sword!" he screamed.

I recoiled in shock and confusion. "What do you mean?"

"Here it is, here!" He riffled through the pages of the Bible until he found Luke chapter 19, verse 27 and read: "But those mine enemies, which would not that I should reign over them, bring hither, and slay them before me."

"Well, I don't believe in Jesus, so go ahead and kill me! See, that's what your Jesus teaches! This is what produced the Spanish Inquisition, the Holocause, anti-Semitism!"

I knew even while he was saying it that it was a parable taken out of context, that it doesn't describe the true nature of God or the love of Jesus. Still, tired and unnerved as I was, I couldn't begin to explain it adequately. With all his yelling and ranting about pogroms and persecutions, and why didn't I just run him through with a sword, I felt totally drained. By the time he left, I was trembling.

The woman, whose name I found out was Susan, had

slipped in quietly with a cheese sandwich and a glass of milk while the man with the Bible was yelling. Amazingly, the ordeal hadn't killed my apetite. I eyed the sandwich longingly, but didn't get to eat it yet.

There was a noise at the door, and another tall, heavy man came in. This was Larry, the one they all called the Boss. Larry wore a big, wide-brimmed hat that well might have earned him the nickname Black Bart in a western movie. Together with the orthodox fringes sticking out from the bottom of his casual pullover shirt, it gave him a rather odd appearance. Larry really scared me. With that big black hat covering his dark hair, tight, grimly set lips dividing his black mustache from his equally black beard, he had a menacing look about him and the towering build of a heavyweight champ.

"C'mon, stand up now," someone said.

I slid off the table and stood there, wondering what would happen next. After the sword episode, I expected more ranting and screaming. Larry's quiet voice took me off guard.

"How ya doin'?"

"Terrible," I sighed. Could it be that he was going to show me some sympathy and kindness?

"Why, what's the matter?" Larry asked. I was beginning to think he sounded over-solicitous.

"I just want to get out of here!"

"Aw," an edge of sarcasm crept into his voice. "Do you know what you're doing here? How did you get here?"

Not sure just what his approach was, I started telling him all about the kidnapping and how badly I had been treated. He glanced over at Susan.

"What a nightmare, what a horror show!" he mocked. "Isn't that terrible?" Susan didn't say anything.

Larry turned to me again. "Have any idea why this happened?"

I shrugged. "I'm not sure."

"Well, why do you think it happened?"

I tried to give him answers I thought he wanted to hear, like my parents being concerned over my faith in Jesus, and things like that. As the conversation progressed, he grew more and more sarcastic and he, too, began to yell and rant and scream at me about what I believed. Susan just stayed in the background, looking angry. I couldn't tell if she was angry with me, or with the way Larry was treating me. Finally Larry finished with me, and I reached hungrily for the sandwich. Susan stretched out her hand.

"Don't forget the blessing!"

"Oh, yeah!" I hastily mumbled the Hebrew benediction praising God for bringing forth bread from the earth. I was used to doing that by then. Since I had been kidnapped, every time I took anything into my mouth, they required me to say the appropriate Hebrew blessing. There was even a special blessing for a drink of water. The only exception was if I were absolutely dying of thirst, then the rule could be waived. Or, if I took a second drink within a certain time after praying over the first drink, I didn't have to pray again. If ever I forgot, someone was right there to remind me.

When at last I was settled with the sandwich, Susan asked, "Would you rather everyone else left so we could talk alone?" I agreed that would be better. After the others left, Susan saw me eyeing the door.

"What're you doing, planning your great escape?"

I didn't answer.

"Well, don't try it," she warned. "You'd never find your way out. You don't even know where you are, and there are people all around the house."

I knew she was telling the truth. I didn't even know my way out of the basement, much less the layout of the house upstairs. They had blindfolded me when they brought me in, and again when I had to be taken to the bathroom. Besides, I was in stocking feet. They had taken away my shoes and belt again.

At first, Susan's tone and manner were sympathetic as we talked.

"So, you believe in Jesus. I can understand why you might think it's true. It gave you purpose in life. It got you a girl friend. . . ." She seemed to know all about Christine and me. That was the first time anyone had mentioned her to me directly.

"I used to be a Christian, too," she went on. "I used to believe all that garbage. I believed it for about seven years, when I was still a kid and into my twenties. I went to church and everything. I was really messed up. But I went through all this a long time ago, and I realized that Christianity isn't real. I had to give up a lot to go back to Judaism, but I did it. You're just afraid to make the sacrifice. You'd rather keep on living a lie than admit you were wrong."

When she finished, others came back in. This new group was even more violent than those in the Boston attic. Among them also was my old tormentor, red-haired Shmuel, the wall-pounder and Bible-thrower. Shmuel also had another device. He would come by with another person, presumably a friend of his. Shmuel would begin to yell and scream at me, and the other fellow would say, "C'mon, cut it out, control yourself! Lay off!" This is known in police interrogation as the Mutt and Jeff tactic, or Good Guy/Bad Guy method. One intimidates, and the other plays a sympathetic role in order to gain the prisoner's confidence and cooperation. I wasn't really aware of this manipulation while it was happening, but I see it now in retrospect.

At one point, Shmuel told me he used to be a Christian. He said he was married to a Gentile girl for about five years and had been divorced within that past year.

Many people who came to talk to me had similar stories about having had relationships with Gentiles that they had severed in order to go back to Judaism.

"We all went through the same thing they said. "We all had to give up a lot to go back to Judaism, but you know, it's worth it. Those relationships never work out anyhow."

They also told me that Shmuel had studied for the Christian ministry at one time, at a seminary. When he went to a Jewish school to study so that he could witness to Jewish people, suddenly he saw the error of his ways, and was converted back to Judaism. I thought that story was a bit far fetched, as were most of the others. It was hard to imagine that the deprogrammers had gone to all the trouble of researching and rounding up all those case histories just to have those people there to impress me.

There were maybe twenty or more people packed into that basement room. Everywhere I looked there were new faces. Sometimes people disappeared and didn't come back; other times they did return. Sometimes the room was almost empty, then it would fill again.

One time when the room had emptied, a second young woman came in. I thought she was in her mid-twenties. She was pregnant. Like Susan, she too, wore a wig to hide her natural hair, and she was carrying a big book.

"Hi, I hear you're going to get married," she began.

"I was supposed to have gotten married yesterday!"

"Well," she said, "before you make any more plans to get married, I'd very much like you to consider having a Jewish wedding."

I didn't think she really knew my whole story, just that she was supposed to talk to me about weddings.

She sat down and opened the book on her lap. "I'd like to show you my pictures. I just recently had a beautiful Jewish wedding."

She started to tell me about the Jewish tradition that every wedding is ordained in heaven twelve days before each partner is born, and began to describe each picture. She even described her family.

Of course looking at the wedding book really made me feel terrible as I remembered missing my own wedding. It was a real psychological squeeze, designed to make me miserable and wear me down.

She left and others came in. They wouldn't leave me alone—to think or sort out my feelings.

Chapter 8

Pressure Is Pain

LORD, why castest thou off my soul? Why hidest thou thy face from me? . . . Lover and friend hast thou put far from me, and mine acquaintance into darkness. (Psalm 88:14, 18)

The basement prison was even worse than the Boston attic. Again, they didn't let me sleep. Even if they had, the narrow cot was broken and very uncomfortable. They took turns screaming verbal abuse at me.

"Nazi! Anti-Semite! How can you believe that God would ever be interested in you or give you a special knowledge of Himself? You're unworthy of His notice. God doesn't deal with men on a personal level. That idea is totally absurd!"

When I raised the question of God relating to our Jewish forefathers, Abraham, Isaac and Jacob in a personal way, and speaking to Moses, they claimed that was different.

"They were completely righteous," the deprogrammers insisted.

I saw it was useless to try to convince them of anything. They didn't want to hear.

Another time Larry looked at Susan and asked, pointing at me, "Do you know what he is?"

"No, don't tell me!" Her response was very dramatic.

"Yup, he is!"

"You're kidding! He's a Levi?"

"That's right!"

She looked disgusted. "He comes from a family of Levites and he's gone astray. What a terrible thing! There aren't too many Levi families left, and they have to be ready to serve in the new temple when the Messiah comes. What a disgrace! He's made himself unfit to serve in the Temple."

All that was meant to make me feel really guilty about abandoning Judaism. They referred to my being a Levi many times in trying to persuade me, and they said all sorts of other things calculated to make me feel miserable and hope-less.

After I had been held in the basement room for a couple of days, Larry suddenly expressed interest in what I had in my pockets.

"Empty your pockets! What do you have there?"

I took everything out. Larry took my wallet. Days later, when I finally got it back, the cards were all messed up, and about sixty or seventy dollars was missing.

I began to lose track of time again. One night the room was even more crowded with tormentors than usual. There were people wherever I looked, maybe as many as twenty-five, and the air was thick with haze because most of them were chain smoking. A man approached me. Though he was beardless, he wore a hat and the orthodox fringes. He spoke with a heavy accent that I thought might be Israeli. In very broken English he started to reprimand me about believing in Jesus. He had a difficult time communicating, but his an-ger and bitterness were unmistakable.

Susan stayed in the thick of it all this time. She had a New American Standard Bible with every New Testament page underlined with what she called "mistakes." She opened it to the first page of Matthew and started showing me these "contradictions." The others chimed in and helped her. When I tried to explain away some of what they said were contradictions, they said, "So you still believe it, huh?"

"Show him this one," a voice would interrupt. Then someone else shouted out another passage, and another, and another, and another, until my head was spinning.

"Open your Bible, Chayim. I want you to read this one!"

"What does that mean, Chayim? Explain it!"

"Explain this one, Chayim. Does that make any sense to you?"

"What do you think about this one, Chayim?"

They kept shouting arguments at me, trying to show me from an intellectual standpoint that the New Testament was ridiculous. I was so tired by then I couldn't answer them any more.

"Well," I admitted, "it *looks* like a contradiction."

"But you still believe it, huh?"

"Yes, I do."

Over and over again they did this, screaming and yelling at me that I was wrong, the Bible was wrong, and I was stupid to believe any of it. They became bitter and violent in their arguments. Susan, too, joined them in shouting, mocking and insulting me, and even throwing things. They said that Jesus was born out of wedlock, the son of Mary and a Roman soldier.

"So you still want to believe?" A New Testament sailed across the room toward me.

The deprogrammers had a stack of Gideon pocket Bibles. They tore pages out of these, lit them, and burned them just inches away from my face.

"What do you see now?" they taunted. "Do you see it yet? Stupid! Can't you get it through your head?"

They looked at each other and wagged their heads. "Boy, this guy's crazy. He's absolutely insane!"

By now I was reeling. It was the worst I had experienced since I was first kidnapped. Horror gripped me as I realized that they might never let me go if I didn't agree with them. Up to that point I had prayed silently that God would deliver me from their clutches. But when I got so fatigued, I began to feel confused and wondered if maybe I had been wrong about Jesus after all. My mind was playing tricks on me. Maybe my captivity and torment was punishment from the God of Israel for believing in a false messiah. I became afraid to pray in Jesus' name anymore, but kept pleading inwardly, "God of Israel, show me the truth. Have I been wrong?"

All the contradictions they were showing me were beginning to get to me. I didn't think it could be like they said, but I just wasn't sure anymore. I didn't realize that my thinking ability was impaired by the lack of sleep and the constant abuse. Slowly I moved toward the intellectual trap they had laid for me. I started to lean on my own understanding without realizing that my confusion was induced by the inhuman treatment I was suffering.

Trembling, I asked my tormentors, "What do you want me to do?"

"Say you don't believe!"

I hedged. "From the information you've given me, it doesn't appear logical that the New Testament is the word of God, and it looks like it might all be made up."

"That's a cop-out! You still believe that garbage! We want to make sure that now you see the truth. We'll stay here for years if it takes that long. We're in no hurry. Say sincerely that you don't believe."

More than anything, I just wanted them to leave me alone. I took a deep breath because I really felt sick. "O.K. I don't believe any more. The New Testament isn't the word of God." I prayed even as I said it, "Oh, God, forgive me if it's true."

I was beginning to believe what the deprogrammers were telling me, and this really frightened me because it was in direct conflict with the reality I had experienced in Christ.

They insisted that I say again that I didn't believe. I repeated the statement.

I heard a voice saying, "Someone go get a tape recorder. We'll record his statement and send it to all the people he knows. We'll make him give us the names and addresses."

Then, suddenly, they became more friendly and less threatening. "Now do you see it? Do you see why we're trying to get this through to you? You've been deceived for two years. We're your friends. Come home! Come home to Judaism. We need you! Your people have a job for you to do."

I was really freaked out. "Yeah, I see it now." I didn't know what I believed anymore.

"Do you feel bad?"

"Yeah."

"Do you feel ashamed?"

I stared miserably at the floor. "I guess so." Part of me still believed that I had been right and had nothing to be ashamed of.

"Do you see that you put your mother through all that stuff for nothing? You ought to feel ashamed! Do you want to repent?"

I shrugged. "I don't know."

"Well, you should," Susan accused.

Larry had gone out, and now he came back with a tape recorder. They read to me from Matthew 10:33: "Whosoever shall deny me before men, him will I also deny before my Father which is in heaven."

"You denied him, didn't you?"

"Yes." My voice shook with shame and exhaustion. I didn't see anyone trying to tape what I said. I just wished they'd all go away and leave me to my misery. I think they knew I was at the point of falling apart, and they did leave me alone for a while to sleep.

When I woke up several hours later, I saw Susan sitting there, watching me.

"So, how's your faith in Jesus?" she asked, halfway sincere and halfway sarcastically.

Shamefully I lied. "I . . . don't believe in Him anymore." I think it was obvious to her that I was having trouble saying it.

"I don't believe you, Chayim. You're lying!"

"What do you mean?" I asked.

"You still believe in Him. None of the things we showed you last night made any impression. It went right through, didn't it? It didn't make any sense to you, no difference at all."

When I heard her say that, I knew she was telling the truth. I did still believe.

"I can't answer your questions," I told her wearily, "but I can't deny that I've had a real experience with God."

Susan spent that whole day talking to me and studying the Old and New Testaments with me.

Once she asked, "What're you going to do? Where are you going to go as soon as you get out of here? Where's the first place you'll go . . . besides the police, that is?"

"I'm not going to the police," I said. I didn't want to have anything more to do with the deprogrammers. If they'd just let me go, I'd decided, I'd leave them alone. "I'll just go home," I told her.

Susan wouldn't let it rest. She looked at me shrewdly. "You'll go back to Chris, won't you?"

"Well," I hedged, "I'm not sure." I didn't want to say anything to jeopardize my chances of getting out.

But Susan knew better. "Oh, yes you will. You'll go back to her."

"Well, I guess I will."

"And you'll still marry her?"

I hedged again. "Well, I don't know, after all the information you've shown me. . . ."

"Don't lie! You want to get married, right?"

"Well, yeah," I admitted, "I do."

Susan sighed. "None of this stuff made any sense to you. You'd still rather live a lie . . . Well, I'll tell you something else." Her voice lost all semblance of friendliness. "Don't bother going to the police. It wouldn't make any difference because we have a court order to keep you here."

"What court order? What're you talking about?"

"You've been declared incompetent by a psychiatrist."

I thought she must be telling me the truth. Why wouldn't they try? They had gone to such lengths to plan this whole thing. It was true that I had gone for counselling at one time, and they might very well pay the doctor to sign such a paper if it enforced their plans. The most ironic aspect of my going for counselling was that, a long time ago, the doctor had advised me to get away from my parents and be my own person.

While Susan and I were talking, Larry came back. He glared at me. "You're tough! At least you think you're tough."

He looked at Susan. "He's got a martyr complex. He's not going to give it up. He's being a martyr. I know what's goin' through his head. He thinks Jesus is gonna come any second now and rescue him with a band of angels, huh?"

He pointed a finger in my face. "Dontcha? Dontcha think that? Well get it through your head, boychik, He's not comin' because He's dead. He's burnin' in hell! You can give up all your hope. He ain't comin' to get you, now or ever. I've had people like you before. They sit here and wait and wait. And you know what happens? He never comes. But if you want to keep on believin' that garbage . . . Oh, boy. We'll see!"

He turned to Susan again. "That's where he's at right

now. Give him another five days, another ten days, another three months, he might change. He's still at the martyr stage. He still thinks he's gonna get rescued. He's still happy to give his life for it. All that stuff he said last night was lies. Don't believe him."

I panicked when I heard him say "another three months."

They both started screaming at me, "Weren't you lying last night? Tell the truth. We can see right through you."

"Yeah," I admitted. "I was lying."

"You still believe it?"

"Yeah, I do."

Susan gave me a wounded look, as though I had stabbed her, and ran out of the room.

Larry went on. "How can you say you still believe? You denied the man. I heard you. If you believe in Him, dontcha believe what He says, that He who denies Him before men, Him will He deny before the Father? Forget it, boychik, it's all over. You denied Him. You can just throw it all out the window. You think He's gonna come and forgive you.?"

Susan came back a little later, crying. "You really hurt me, Chayim. I thought you were sincere. Why did you lie?"

"Well," I defended myself, "I wanted to stop all of you from screaming at me. I couldn't stand the treatment any more. That's why I lied."

She continued to look wounded. "I've tried so hard to make you see the truth." She stayed and kept talking to me, trying again to persuade me not to believe.

Every so often, Larry came back in to check on my progress. He'd look at me piercingly. "Well, whadd'ya say, boychik? You still wanta believe it dontcha?" He called me "boychik" a lot. The term, when used with anyone except small children, is like the term "boy." It's a way of talking down to someone when the person is no longer a child.

"I want you to tell me what you believe," he'd insist.

When I couldn't tell him what he wanted to hear, more abuse would follow.

I kept asking him, "When are you going to let me go?"

"Oh, don't worry about that," Larry drawled. "You're

gonna stay here a really long time. You're not goin' anywhere! If you ever get out, it won't be for a long time, boychik. By the time you get out, people won't recognize you
any more. They'll have forgotten you."

He also tried to convince me that Christine didn't care
about me any more.

"Your friend there, your little ugly duckling, she's run-
nin' around with some other guy now. She's sleepin' with
him. She doesn't want to see you. You can just forget about
her. She'll probably show up here with her new boyfriend
soon. Maybe she even helped set this whole thing up. She's
probably happy to get rid of you."

I didn't believe any of that. "I just want to write her a letter, or talk to her," I pleaded.

"Oh, you can forget about her! She got a letter from you,
and the things you said in that letter show her that you don't
want to have anything to do with her any more. It's not a very
nice letter, Chayim. After she's read that, she hates you."

That really added to my misery. I had agonized so much
already over missing the wedding, wondering if Christine
had any idea of what had happened to me, if she even knew
if I was alive or dead. I knew these people who had me might
stoop to anything. It was easily believable to me that they had
really written Christine a hate letter from me. I thought if they
had, she probably wouldn't believe it, but I couldn't be sure. I
felt so helpless. Wouldn't they ever let me go? Why didn't
someone find me? I was close to the breaking point.

Chapter 9

Horror Show

For days I saw nothing but the walls of my basement prison. They still blindfolded me to go to the bathroom, and someone was always guarding me. Those four white walls with their sparse, ugly furnishings were my only world, my only reality, those hostile, angry people my only human contact.

When I had been there for three or four days, maybe Wednesday night or very early Thursday morning, they set up movie equipment on one of the high utility tables and forced me to watch a film about the Holocaust. It was a gruesome documentary about the most inhuman, disgusting atrocities imaginable. It showed Jewish women and children in the concentration camps being herded into gas chambers, heaps of naked emaciated corpses, already skeletons even before they died, stacks of lampshades and bars of soap made from human skin and body fat—a panorama to sicken even the most stout of heart.

I had seen this film at least twice before in my life. It's often used by Jewish educational institutions to impress people with the threat of anti-Semitism and the need for Jewish unity. Knowing already what was in that film, I steeled myself for the most grisly parts. Still, I couldn't help but react to some degree. I knew everyone was watching me, and it was hard to know whether I should hide my feelings or exaggerate them. After the film, they accused me of being anti-Semitic and uncaring.

"Your face stayed stone-cold throughout the whole film," they said. "You have no feelings. You're a sickie! You need to be put away. It's not safe to have you out on the streets. You're no better than an animal, and you deserve to die. Even if you say now you've changed your mind about Jesus, we won't believe you. We'd do well just to get rid of you. If we let you go and you marry that *shicksa* (Gentile), you'll have children that will grow up to be Christian murderers like the Nazis. They'll kill our own innocent children in another holocaust, just like Germany. We'll see to it that you don't marry her!"

That sounded to me like a veiled threat. Maybe they hadn't really sent Christine that hate letter because they still seemed worried about my marrying her. Now I began to worry that they might try to kidnap her, too, and do something terrible to her.

After the movie they made me stand up and count dead babies. "Christians murder Jews!" they yelled at me. "By believing in Jesus, you've become a murderer, too. You've killed innocent Jewish children. Name a kid!"

"No," I protested.

"Name a kid! A boy's name!"

I didn't know what they might do to me if I didn't, so I thought of a boy's name and said it.

"What'd he look like? How old was he?" They kept screaming at me until I answered something.

"Now, how did you kill him?"

"I didn't kill anyone," I protested again.

"HOW DID YOU KILL IT?"

I knew they wouldn't leave me alone until I said something. I said I beat the child, or kicked it. Then they wanted me to describe the torture. "Do it! Show us how you did it!" They were really getting off on the subject—and they said *I* was sick.

"No, I can't," I exploded. "I told you, I didn't kill anyone. Leave me alone!"

"Name a girl now!"

The only name I could think of was my sister's name, Sheryll.

"That's not a Jewish name," someone yelled. If the whole thing hadn't been so sick and frightening, that would have been very funny.

"How did you kill this one? Did you put her on the end of a bayonet and lift her up?"

I don't remember my answer. I could only stand there and hope they would stop.

Susan came over to me. "Do you know what a baby is? Do you want to see some babies?"

She went out and came back leading a little boy by the hand. He must have been five or six years old and he was in his pajamas.

"Say hello to Chayim." The kid looked at me with big eyes, afraid to say anything. Susan sent him off with a kiss goodnight and brought in another little boy. This one looked younger, maybe only two or three. He, too, was in his night-clothes and looked scared. I wondered if they had told these kids that I was crazy, or a murderer or something, or maybe they were just naturally shy.

Susan also carried in a very young infant. She wouldn't let me touch it. Her voice was choked with emotion. "Babies like this you want to murder!"

After Susan left, they kept me standing there. "Name Jewish babies killed by the hand of Jesus." I didn't want to, but they forced me.

"One Jewish baby," I began. "Two Jewish babies, three...."

"NO!" they shouted. "Say, 'Jewish babies killed by the hand of Jesus.'"

Their mood was too ugly for me to resist. "O.K., one Jewish baby killed by the hand of Jesus, two Jewish babies killed by the hand of Jesus, three Jewish babies...."

Every time I tried to stop counting, they screamed at me to keep on counting. They didn't let me stop until I had counted like that to fifteen hundred.

Even after I finished, they wouldn't leave me alone. Things got progressively worse, and Larry came back in.

"Well, boychik, where do we go from here? It's your choice now. So what're we gonna do? You want to go to a mental institution? I don't think you need to go to a yeshiva to study Judaism, I think you need psychiatric help!" He looked at the others. "So what'll we do with him?"

"You're gonna go on a long trip, Chayim, and you ain't never gonna come back. When your friend sees you, she ain't never gonna recognize you because you're gonna look like those pictures in that movie. You'll look worse than that! No one will know you when we get through with you.

"You're gonna be flown out of here, and I'm not the one who's gonna do it. No sir, I don't handle that stuff. Those are some other people. And the other people, you know, they're not as nice as I am. You think this is bad? You ain't seen nuthin' yet. You're gonna be so far away nobody is ever gonna see you again. Nobody! And you're gonna wish you never were alive. We're gonna take you for a little trip. Someone's gonna be there, but you're not gonna like seeing her. You're gonna watch what's gonna happen to her!"

Through the haze of my weariness and despair, that last phrase cut like a knife into my consciousness. The seed of fear the deprogrammers had managed to plant in my mind about Christine's safety blossomed into full terror. What had he meant by "You're gonna watch what's gonna happen to her"?

Later, in one of my talks with Susan, I told her that Larry had threatened to have Christine raped or tortured in front of me if I didn't shape up. Larry came in the next day, looking serious and upset.

"What did you say to Susan about Christine?"

"That you threatened to have her raped or tortured in front of me if I didn't give in."

Larry raised his eyebrows and frowned. "Did I say that?"

"Well, yeah, that's the impression I got from you."

He shook his head. "I'm sorry if that's what you heard. I didn't mean to make you think that." He left the room.

I was somewhat relieved, but still I didn't trust him or any of the others. As violent as they had been with me, I could visualize them doing anything, saying anything, to accomplish their goals.

I hadn't slept for so long, I was dizzy, depressed, and spacing out. Still, the deprogrammers kept shouting at me to give up my faith, quoting Bible verses that were supposed to be mistakes, wanting me to give them answers. They burned Bibles in my face again. They wouldn't let me sit down any more, and I had to stand there while they crumpled up more pages from the pocket testaments and stuffed them into my ears and mouth. At that point, I hardly knew my name, let alone anything else. I was sweating and shaky. All I could do was repeat, "I want to get out! You've got to let me out of here!"

"Oh, man, don't worry about getting out," they taunted. "You're not going anywhere for a while."

I got more and more upset. "You can't keep me here forever!"

Larry reinforced his previous threats. "If you ever get out, it won't be for a long time! People aren't going to recognize you when you get out. They'll have forgotten you by then." I really believed he meant that.

By now it felt like morning. I could see that the deprogrammers looked tired, too. An absolute blanket of horror and despair had settled over me and I thought I couldn't go on like this another minute.

"What do I have to do to get out?" I begged.

"Renounce Him!"

I felt really sick, and I just wanted to get it over with. "O.K., I don't believe it any more."

"NO! Say 'Jesus is not the Messiah, and I don't believe.' "

I wanted to die. "Jesus is not the Messiah, and I don't believe," I repeated hollowly.

"If you don't believe, why is it so hard for you to say it?" Larry asked. He handed me a piece of paper and made me write the verse from Matthew: "He who denies me before men, him will I deny before my father in heaven."

"Now sign it," he demanded.

I scrawled my name.

"Now confess again before us all that you don't believe in Jesus any more!"

I nodded assent, praying inwardly, "Oh God, forgive me if you're real." Right then, tormented, intimidated, ragged from only eight or nine hours of sleep over the span of a week, I would have said anything, signed anything, just to have peace and to be let go. Later, I confessed my denial as sin, and felt reassured that God had forgiven me, but then I felt utterly hopeless.

The deprogrammers seemed temporarily appeased, but

not fully convinced. They began to make suggestions about my future plans.

"Now what? Do you think you can pick up the pieces of your shattered life?" Susan asked.

I was really depressed. "I don't know."

They brought up the idea of my studying at a Jewish school in Israel. I really didn't want to do that, but I went along with them and didn't protest.

The deprogrammers began to soften toward me. They let me go upstairs without a blindfold, and even allowed me to sit in the back yard for about an hour. They watched me the whole time, but they really didn't need to. I wore no shoes, had no belt, and my pants were falling down from all the weight I had lost. When I came inside the deprogrammers gave me back my shoes and belt and a suitcase full of clean clothes. The suitcase looked new, and I didn't recognize any of the clothes, except for one old sweater I remembered leaving at my parents' house months before. Also in the case were my electric razor, my wallet containing only paper money, no change, my car keys, and my grandfather's old Jewish prayer book. I had the feeling my mother had packed it for me.

"Oh, man," I thought. "No wonder she couldn't meet my eyes the morning we talked at the apartment. She must have helped plan the whole thing!"

Then they let me have a shower, the first I had had in a week and a half. I felt like I'd never get clean again. It was Friday afternoon. I knew that because I saw them preparing for the sabbath. Everyone dressed up, and for the first time, I sat at a table to eat with them. Suddenly, they were treating me like a guest. I thought they were trying to win me back to Judaism by showing me the beauty of keeping the sabbath. It was very nice, but it didn't seem to have anything to do with the issue of the messiahship of Jesus. After the sabbath meal, they let me have a full night's sleep. They were suddenly treating me very nicely.

After the sabbath they asked, "How would you like to call Chris?"

I couldn't believe their offer. Larry set up an extra phone

in the kitchen and took off the mouthpiece. He sat down with me and dialed the number and listened to the whole conversation. He told me to keep it brief. If I hadn't, they were ready to disconnect.

"Hello, Chris? It's me, Ken."

Hearing her voice was almost like coming home.

"Ken! Where are you?"

"I'm sorry, I can't tell you."

Chris sounded worried. "Are you O.K.? Who has you?"

"I'm O.K. . . . "

"Has anybody hurt you?"

"No, they're nice. . . . " I was afraid to say anything else.

"Ken, is someone listening?"

"Yeah, they are."

"When can I see you? When are you coming back?"

"Chris. . . . " Larry looked at me sternly and held up a piece of paper on which he had written "Only thirty seconds more!"

"Chris, I have to go now. Don't worry, I'm O.K. I'll be back soon."

They would have disconnected the call if I hadn't finished.

They arranged for me to be taken to a place in the country to recuperate.

"It'll be like a vacation," they told me. "You'll be outdoors, no one will bother you, and you'll have time to think about what you want to do with your life. We'll even bring your girlfriend up to see you if you like."

In the morning they got me ready to leave. This time when the deprogrammers brought me out of the house where I was held, they didn't blindfold me. When I walked out into the sun, I felt like I had just come back from a distant planet. It was a beautiful world out there, but I was too numb to feel very much a part of it.

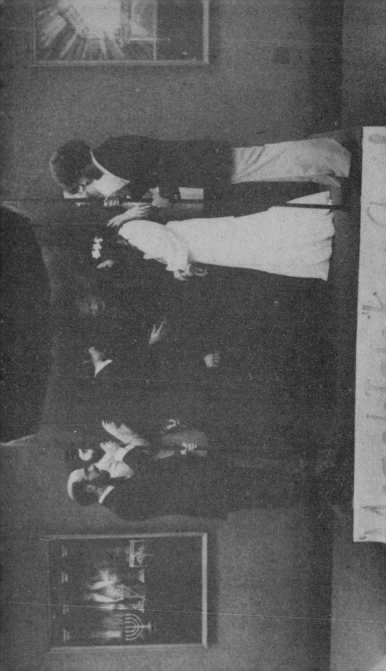

Chapter 10

There are Goats in the Country

Outside the house where I had been kept prisoner the deprogrammers had a blue station wagon waiting. They put me in the middle seat. Shmuel drove, and his young wife and son and two others, Kalman and Shoshana, rode with us.

"Keep your head down and don't look out of the windows until we say you can," they instructed.

Why were they still being so careful about not letting me know where I was? Was everything as kosher and legal as Susan had implied? I began to wonder.

After about fifteen minutes of driving through stop-and-go traffic, we got onto what felt like a major highway. Now they let me look out of the windows. I saw cars with New York license plates, but the highway signs were unfamiliar until I saw one that read "Cross Island Expressway." Then I guessed that they had been holding me somewhere on Long Island.

After awhile I saw signs giving directions to Brooklyn, and we took that turnoff. Some of the people in the wagon with us lived there and needed rides home. After we dropped them off, the deprogrammers took me to a yeshivah (Jewish religious school) in Brooklyn. They kept me waiting in one of the rooms in the adminstration office while they made some telephone arrangements. Finally someone came in to get me.

"Well, it's all set now," he told me. "We're taking you up to the country. Do you like goats? Did you ever milk one? It's quiet up there. You'll be able to rest and relax and get your head together."

They put me back in the station wagon. Shmuel was driving again, and Kalman and two of the yeshivah students came along. The drive from New York City to the Catskills takes a few hours. Once out on the Throughway, we passed some beautiful scenery, but I still felt too exhausted and numb to care much. It was Memorial Day weekend, and the road was thick with cars and campers; happy, carefree people on vacation; families in station wagons with bouncy, exuberant kids in the back seats; dogs with their heads out of the windows, fur and tongue streaming in the breeze; people on motorcycles; couples in compact cars sitting very close to each other. I looked at those couples enviously. It was May 28th, a week after Chris and I were to have been married. We should have been one of those happy couples now, riding along a mountain road, headed for a camp site. And those families in the station wagons and campers! Their most pressing problem was probably no more complicated than finding the next gas station so the kids could have a bathroom stop. "Hey, people," I thought. "What would you think if you knew what I've been through these past ten days? Could you relate to that? Would you even believe it really happened?" I felt very much alone, and very miserable.

Late in the afternoon we neared our destination. In the Greenfield Park/Ellenville area, I saw a sign that read "Camp Emunah." How ironic it was that *emunah* means "faith" in Hebrew. As we approached the camp grounds, I saw green, rolling hills and thick forests. The camp itself was very attractive, with low buildings that were rustic in appearance, but had modern conveniences. There was also a farm area with goats, chickens, and a vegetable garden.

They introduced me to the caretaker. His name was Frank Leavitt, almost like my name, but he spelled his with "ea" instead of just "e." He must be a Levi, too, I thought. Well, there was one representative of the priestly tribe who hadn't "gone astray" from Judaism! Frank was in his late thirties, maybe about thirty-seven. He always had his head covered with either a skull cap or some kind of hat. His face above his full black beard was tanned from working out in the sun, and his casual shirt over blue jeans didn't come down long enough to hide the ritual fringes he wore underneath. When I first met him, he was puffing on a cigarette, and he had one dangling from the side of his mouth almost every time I saw him. Frank's wife was a small, thin girl. She looked younger than Frank. They introduced her by a Hebrew name, but I don't remember what it was. She was orthodox, too, and always had her head covered with a green terry towel tied at the nape of her neck. They were pleasant enough, and welcomed me. I wondered if they knew my whole story.

Then Frank showed me to my sleeping quarters. The modern, air conditioned cabin looked like counsellors' quarters, with four beds, two at one end of the room, and two more at the other end. I set my suitcase down by one of the beds.

After I was settled, they gave me freedom to roam the camp grounds as I pleased, but I was being closely watched. I didn't know this at first, but I realized it when I decided that first night to take a walk by myself before bedtime. As I opened the door and stepped out into the evening air, there was a voice at my elbow.

"Hey, Chayim, where are you goin'?" The two yeshivah students were standing in the doorway.

I was startled. "I thought I'd just take a short walk before going to sleep."

"Well, we'll come along and keep you company." Suddenly, I had two unsolicited "pals" to keep me from getting lonely and to make sure I didn't get "lost."

"So," I thought, "I'm still a prisoner!" I wasn't thinking of running away anyhow right then. I still more or less believed what Susan had said about the police bringing me back if I tried to escape. Also, I was still confused about God, and welcomed the time to think.

I had another reason, too, for not trying to escape just yet. They kept promising to bring Christine up to see me, but they still hadn't finalized any arrangements for her visit. I was afraid that if I ran away, she would come and not find me. But, when they kept delaying Christine's visit, that got me thinking.

"Why is it taking so long?" I asked Pinchas one day. I was still relating to him much better than any of the others. I found out his real name was Fishel, and Pinchas was just an alias during the deprogramming. He said, "Don't worry, just relax. She'll be up soon enough."

Another time, I asked Frank. "Well," he explained, "they've go to be careful in order to protect themselves."

Protect themselves from what? Suddenly, with my head a bit clearer, it dawned on me. They really were keeping me there illegally. They had no court order! From that moment I started to think seriously about how and when I would escape.

Wednesday, the fourth night I was at Camp Emunah, Larry called. It sounded like a long distance call because his voice was faint and there was static on the line. I also heard beeps that sounded like he was taping the conversation.

"So how's your little *keppeleh?*" he asked me. That's the Yiddish word for little head. "Are you depressed?" Everyone was always asking me was I depressed and how was my head doing.

"Yeah," I admitted. "I'm not at all happy up here."

"So whaddya wanna do? You call the shots now. It's your ball game. I know that even if we let you out tonight, you'd still know we're right. I think our job's done. We only wanted to show you the truth, and now it's all up to you."

"They're asking me if I want to go to Israel," I said. "I definitely don't want to go to Israel."

"So, don't go to Israel. What do you want to do instead? What're you planning to do when you leave?"

"I just want to go home to Boston and get things straightened out about Chris."

"Are you still gonna marry her?" I thought I detected a sharp edge to his voice.

"Well," I countered, "I just want to talk to her. I owe her that much. But if God let all this happen to me and brought me here because He doesn't want me to believe in Jesus, then I guess He doesn't want me to marry Chris, either."

The deprogrammers had managed to plant just enough doubt in my mind that I really wasn't sure if my ordeal was punishment from God or not. I couldn't shake the terrible feeling that maybe He had made it all happen because I wasn't supposed to believe in Jesus, after all. Still, I felt I wanted to marry Chris, anyhow. On the other hand, if my doubts were true, God might punish me even more for marrying a Gentile. Sometimes I would think, "Oh, just forget about God and marry her anyhow." Other times, I got very frightened.

Still, Larry was right to be concerned about my going back to Boston. These people were shrewd. I think he sensed that even if I doubted God, I'd probably end up marrying Chris. I told Larry that I knew that if God wasn't in the relationship, then I shouldn't marry Chris. But all the time I was wanting to marry her, regardless of anything else.

Whether he believed me or not, Larry knew enough to hold out some hope to me about seeing Chris soon. "Well," he promised, "we'll see what we can do about arranging a meeting." Then he told Frank to let me call Chris that night to see if she wanted to come up.

Frank got her on the phone and let me talk, but he stayed in the room, listening. Every once in a while he held up a slip of paper saying how many minutes were left for me to talk.

Chris sounded miserable and desperate. She asked when I would be free. I told her I didn't know, but she should do whatever they said if they tried to make arrangements for her to come. I thought it might be an opportunity for me to escape.

The night before, Fishel, whose name in Long Island was Pinchas, was guarding me. They still never left me by myself, especially at night. I woke up the next morning and couldn't find my clothes. Fishel had taken my pants, shoes, and belt when I went to bed, and hid them so I wouldn't try to leave.

When I confronted him and asked why, he said, "I just wanted to make sure nothing happened while I was watching you."

The others weren't being that careful any more. I wondered if something in my behavior or in my face had clued him to the thoughts of escape that were building up inside me.

Chapter 11
Miracle Dime

"... thou, O LORD, art a God full of compassion, and gracious, longsuffering, and plenteous in mercy and truth.

O turn unto me and have mercy upon me; give thy strength unto thy servant ... shew me a token for good..." (Psalm 86:15-17)

Fishel and I were out on the lake in a rowboat. We drifted for a while, enjoying the water and the sun, and we talked. Everyone talked to me now in a more or less friendly manner, and we did things together, like playing Monopoly, boating, and hiking through the grounds. Frank even took me away from the campground to a small morning synagogue service in town, but my "companions" always came along, too.

Fishel trailed his fingers through the water, "So you and I are going to Israel Saturday night, huh?"

That again! "I don't think I want to go to Israel just now." I tried to sound more casual than I felt.

"Oh, c'mon, why don't you go? I think it's divine providence that I'm going now, because I have someone to go with me. I really didn't want to go alone. I think we'd have a good time together. I've got a cousin who has a pilot's license, and he can fly us all over the place. It'll be great!"

"Well, let me think about it, but I don't think so." I was hardly enthused. All I needed was for these people to spirit me out of the country, and I'd probably never get back. Even while Fishel was talking about the great time we'd have, my mind was busy devising schemes for escaping from Israel, if it should come to that. The idea of being held prisoner in a foreign country really frightened me. Long Island was bad enough. And no matter how nice they were acting toward me, I *was* still their prisoner.

I brought my mind back to what Fishel was saying. "Yeah," he went on. "I guess they're going to bring Christine up pretty soon, like they promised. It would have to be soon if we're leaving on Saturday."

Excitement stirred within me, but I tried not to act too enthused. I had a feeling that these people could outguess me, and right now I was thinking if they did arrange a meeting between Chris and me, it would be easier for me to escape. Because they didn't want Chris to know exactly where I was being held, they would have to arrange the meeting in some more public place than the camp. This would make them more vulnerable, and their hold on me would be far less secure.

For days I had been so confused and guilt-ridden, I was afraid to pray any more in Jesus' name. But now my mind and body were growing stronger, and I couldn't discount the experience I had with Christ for the past two years.

I prayed, "Jesus, if you're real, and you forgive me, and you want me to escape, show me a sign. Let me find a dime for a phone call."

I was frightened even as I prayed. I still had the vague uneasiness that maybe God was punishing me and didn't want me to get away. He knew my weakness and doubt and made it easy for me. Within an hour, Jesus answered my prayer!

A few of us were standing around outside, just talking and relaxing, when a girl called out, "Hey look! I found a dime on the ground. Anyone want it?" She was one of the people the deprogrammers had brought up from the city to help guard me.

Everyone said no, they didn't want the dime. Then she turned to me.

"Chayim, do you want it?"

I shook my head. "No, thanks." My heart was thumping, and I didn't dare show my desperation to have it.

"Go on, take it!" she urged.

I tried very hard to sound nonchalant. "Well, O.K., if you insist." I held out my hand, hoping she wouldn't see how I was shaking.

There in the palm of my hand lay a small, grubby, mud-caked coin. To me that stained bit of silver alloy wasn't a symbol of United States currency, but a token of God's eternal love and forgiveness. Though in a weak moment I had denied Him, He still loved me, and He had answered my prayer!

Later, we were all in the kitchen having lunch, and somehow I dropped that precious dime on the floor. My heart sank. I didn't dare make a dive for it, or they'd guess and take it away. I followed it with my eyes, marking the place where it stopped. I made sure no one was looking before I carefully retrieved it and slipped it into my pocket. Now I had the means to use a pay phone! All I had to do was leave the grounds and find a telephone.

It was now Thursday evening, two full weeks from that night I was blindfolded, tied up, and dragged from my parents' house in Newton, when finally I saw my chance for a step toward freedom! In all the time I was staying at Camp Emunah, the people who were guarding me never left me alone. Now, for the first time, I found myself all alone in the sleeping cabin. If I ever hoped to sneak out of that cabin while my guards slept, I would have to fix the door. It squeaked loudly at the slightest touch, and I knew I could never open it without waking someone.

With trembling fingers, I grabbed a bar of soap and wet it from the slow trickle of the tap. I made a sudsy solution in the soap dish and carefully poured the stuff over and around the rusty hinges. It dripped to the floor in a puddle, but I hastily mopped it up. Good! Nothing looked at all unusual, but now a new worry nagged at me. Would they notice that the squeaky door was suddenly quiet? Then they would guess my plan to escape. Somehow, praise God, they didn't notice.

Two nights before, Fishel had taken my pants, shoes, and belt. I had to make sure that didn't happen again. Even if I could run barefoot, I couldn't get far without pants and belt. I climbed into bed with all my clothes on, and pulled the blanket up high under my chin so nothing showed. Then I went to sleep as the first shift of guards came in and went to bed. One lay right beside me, not three feet away. The others were at the far end of the room.

Just before I went to sleep, Frank came in and told me, "I think they're bringing Christine up on Sunday."

That confirmed in my mind that this was the night I should escape. There was no danger of her coming up earlier and missing me if I left.

About one o'clock in the morning, the second shift came in. The noise of their voices woke me, and I stayed awake, pretending to be asleep. After what seemed like an eternity, I heard slow, steady breathing all around me, and I figured they were all asleep. Slowly I sat up, swung one leg over the side of the bed, and groped for the floor with my foot. The fellow in the bed right next to me stirred. He sat up and looked at me, eyes vacant with sleep. I froze. Then, miraculously, he flopped back down on his bed and was snoring soundly. The other two, at their end of the room, also were dead to the world.

I inched my body off the narrow cot. In the warm, still air of the cabin my fingers were cold and clammy as they found the suitcase handle by the bed. With hammering heart I made my way to the cabin door. Would it squeak? It swung open, smooth as silk. As I tiptoed over the threshold, my stomach lurched. There, right by the door, was Shmuel, but he, too, was sleeping soundly. It was as though God had shut my guards' eyes for me, just as He shut the lions' mouths for Daniel. My knees were shaking as I heel-toed past that last guard, one painfully slow step at a time. At last, I was clear of the buildings. Then, suitcase and all, I bolted to freedom. I didn't stop running until I felt my lungs would burst. Then I slowed to a fast walk, but I didn't dare stop. They had me so brainwashed, I was still struggling with the fear that I wasn't only running from the deprogrammers, but from God Himself.

Alternately walking and running, the suitcase bumping against my bruised and weary legs, I managed to put about five miles between me and Camp Emunah. Two cars passed but didn't stop when I held out my thumb. At the intersection of Routes 52 and 209, I found a gas station. The station was closed for the night, but there was a phone booth. Its smudged windows, graffiti covered walls, and frayed telephone book were the most beautiful sight I had seen for two weeks. Shaking with fatigue and tension, I fumbled for my miracle dime and put through a collect call to Christine. I didn't have to tell her I'd been kidnapped. She'd known all along that only something that drastic would have kept me from our wedding. I explained about my escape and asked her to call the Ellenville police.

"I'm going to try to hitchhike to Boston," I told her.

Then I started running again. I wanted to get as far away as possible from the camp before they woke and realized I was gone.

I ran until I was out of breath and slowed to a walk. A beam of headlights pierced the pre-dawn darkness, and I waved the car down. The fellow took me only a few more miles down the road before dropping me off, and I continued my flight. I had told him I'd been kidnapped, but he didn't seem to care.

I felt like a hunted animal. Any minute, I thought, a car would come down the road looking for me. I kept on going until I saw an old house set back from the road at the edge of a woodsy area. Panting with fatigue, I pounded on the door. A dog started yapping from somewhere inside, and an old man came to the door. He was dressed, but his face, puffy from sleep, betrayed the uneasiness he felt as he looked at me through the screen.

I held up my driver's license and told him my name.

"I've been kidnapped, and just escaped! Please help me! Could I use your phone to call the police, or could you call them for me?" I pleaded.

Several missing front teeth muffled his words, but his message was plain enough.

"You gid away f'm here . . . Don' wan' no trouble, don' wanna gid involved. Da police come downa road alla time, dey'll help you."

"Couldn't I just use your telephone?"

"Naw, I don' wanna have anythin' t'do widdis. You better go."

I was desperate. "How about the people next door? Who lives there?"

"Jus' some kids. Don' wake 'em up. They're probably sleepin' and don' wan' anythin' t'do widdis either." He closed the door in my face.

I ran next door. It was a very weird little house, old, with piles of junk in the yard and padlocks on the front door. It didn't look like anyone lived there. I pounded on the door, but no one answered.

The old man stuck his head out of his front door and yelled, "C'mon, gid away now. Dey don' wanna have anythin' t'do widdis. Police'll be comin' downa road soon. Gid oudah here!"

I started down a crossroad I found and kept knocking on doors, ringing doorbells. No one answered. By now it was light and cars were coming down the road. I waited until they passed and ran across the road. Every time I heard a car, I'd hide behind some bushes and look to see if it was Frank Leavitt's big black truck. After I made sure it wasn't, I'd run out in the road and try to wave a car down. When they saw me waving at them wildly, I'd hear them accelerate and they'd zoom off in a hurry.

"Well," I thought, "I'll stay and hide in the bushes for days if I have to. I'll never let them find me again, no matter what." I figured they couldn't keep looking for me forever. Sooner or later, they'd have to give up, and I was determined to outwait them.

Chapter 12
Help!

Despite my determination to find help, I was getting wearier by the minute. I stayed on the side road for a while, plodding along, hoping for a ride or someone who might aid me. I saw another car coming. This one had a uniformed driver, maybe a mailman or a security cop. I got to it just as it passed me, and I ran after it, waving my arms and yelling. The car kept right on going.

I was running through a residential section now, and I went up to two houses and pounded on the doors. No one answered. The next one was a good sized white colonial. I tried again. This time I heard a dog barking loudly. A woman came to the door. I saw her through the window, tying her robe around her as she groped her way down the stairs. She had a big, mean-looking police dog with her. Her voice was as disgruntled as her face as she opened the door a crack.

"What's going on down here? What do you want?"

I opened the screen door and held up my driver's license for her to see.

"My name's Kenneth Levitt. I've just escaped from kidnappers. I was being held at a camp up the road in Ellenville, and I wonder if I could use your phone to call the police."

"Get outa here!" She was disgusted, angry, unbelieving. The dog got excited at the tone of her voice, and his low, rumbling growl turned again to insistent barking. The woman backed away from the door and started to close it in my face.

I stretched out my hand despairingly and looked her right in the eye.

"Please," I protested, "I'm telling you the truth!"

She took another step backward and stopped. Her expression changed, and the hand that was about to slam the door froze in mid-air. I put my driver's license up to the screen again, and this time she looked at it. It was hard to recognize me from my picture because I had grown a beard while I was being held. For two weeks I hadn't had any razor at all. They wouldn't give me one because it was some kind of a special Jewish fasting period when one didn't shave, and by the time they gave me the suitcase with my electric shaver, my beard was too heavy to use it. Still, I could see the woman was beginning to believe me.

"Please, may I call the police?"

She still didn't want to let me inside, but she opened the door and took my driver's license.

"Don't come in," she warned. "The dog's pretty mean. You wait there and I'll call them for you. State police or local police?"

"State," I told her.

By now a teenage girl in shorts had wandered downstairs and was watching curiously. I assumed she was the woman's daughter.

The woman hushed the big dog and started to make the phone call. As she was dialing, her husband, too, came down the stairs. His huge frame filled the doorway.

"What the devil's goin' on down here?" I guess I looked rather grisly, and he was upset to think this disheveled, bleary-eyed guy with an unkempt beard and frantic manner might be threatening his family.

I repeated my story. "I was kidnapped from Boston two weeks ago, and I was being held at a camp just down the road from here. I just escaped, and I need to call the police."

As I spoke, his wife handed him my driver's license. He peered at it, then at me, still looking skeptical and a bit puzzled. He cocked his head at me.

"So . . . you were kidnapped, huh?"

I nodded. "I've been running all night, and I couldn't find anyone to help me."

He gestured toward his wife. "Well, she's calling the police, and they'll be here any minute."

He sent the woman and the girl back upstairs and stayed to talk with me in the doorway. As I unfolded all the details of my ordeal, he became more friendly.

He shook his head sympathetically. "Boy, that's really crazy. I don't know why the police are taking so long. They're just down the street here in Wurtsboro."

The woman came back dressed, and went off to work.

"Am I keeping you from going to work, too?" I asked her husband.

"No, I'm not going until later. Would you like a cup of coffee?"

"No, thanks." I was too nervous.

At last the police car from the Wurtsboro station drove up. Only one officer was on duty. After the man introduced himself and told him who I was, the policeman took me down to the patrol car. He questioned me about a robbery and beating that had taken place down the road the night before. I couldn't believe he was suspecting me of a crime when I had called him as the victim of a kidnapping. After I satisfied him that I was nowhere near the scene of the crime and didn't even know where the place was, he got back to my kidnapping story. I told him I thought there was an APB out on me in Boston from two weeks ago, and he checked that out in his file. Pinchas had mentioned this to me earlier as the reason for my being moved from Boston to Long Island.

"There's nothing about you in the files," the officer now told me, "but these are only local. You didn't make the national computer if there was an APB out on you. Come on down to the station. It'll take a while, but we'll find out."

I told him some of the other details of what had happened to me as we drove back in the patrol car. What a relief it was to sink down in the seat and feel that I could stop running, at last.

My story was so incredible that the police could hardly believe it. While they were questioning me, Christine was praying for me in Boston, not quite sure as to what she should do. As she was praying, an investigator from the Wurtsboro station called her to verify my bizarre story.

"How long will Ken be there at the station?" Chris asked the investigator. "I'd like to drive over to see him."

"He's not going very far for a while," the investigator told her. "He's talking to the Ellenville police right now, but he'll be at the Middletown station."

Chris decided to drive up right away. She told the inspector, "Please just make sure he stays till I get there."

Christine grabbed her suitcase, already packed for our honeymoon. She hastily packed a few things for me and put my suit and the ill-fated wedding dress in a garment bag. The Jews for Jesus office had warned her, when she told them what was happening, not to come back to Boston with me. They thought I might be in danger there. They had also suggested that we get married as soon as possible. My parents had already gone to such lengths, they might try, as next of kin, to get me declared mentally incompetent. They could get the deprogrammers to testify that I had lost my sanity. On the other hand, if Christine were my wife, they wouldn't be able to do that because then she would be my next of kin. That might sound far-fetched to some people who read this, but there have been instances where perfectly sane Jewish Christians have spent weeks, months, and even years in institutions at the instigation of their zealous but misguided families.

With all these thoughts racing through her mind, Christine made ready to leave Boston. My roommate Greg was out of town and had left her the keys to his car. She tossed the luggage in back and headed for upstate New York. Meanwhile, the New York City Jews for Jesus office was sending one of their people, Steve Cohen, to Middletown, too. He would arrive before Chris, because he had the shorter drive.

Chris had a long drive ahead of her. Excited and thankful for answered prayers, she wished somehow that she could shorten the seven-hour trip. As she drove along, the heartaches and uncertainty of the past ten days flashed in painful sequence through her thoughts.

She remembered the evening of the wedding rehearsal. She had waited at the apartment with my friend Steve, and

Ellen, her roommate. They were our wedding attendants, and we were to go to the rehearsal together. When it started to get late and I still hadn't picked them up at the apartment, Steve called my parents' house.

"Oh," they said. "Ken just left a little while ago."

I had left all right, in the kidnap van! But they didn't tell him that.

When it got later and later, they all began to worry about me. They thought I might have gotten into an accident, or, because my car needed some repairs, it had broken down somewhere. Still, if I were safe I would most certainly call and explain the delay. When they didn't hear from, they became very concerned.

Steve and Ellen told our pastor that the rehearsal was postponed because I was missing. The pastor was upset because he had received a threatening phone call supposedly from a member of the Jewish Defense League the previous week. He prayed with them and made them promise to keep him informed as soon as they heard anything.

When at 11:30 p.m. they still had no word from me, Chris called the police and Jeff, the leader of our Jews for Jesus Boston Bible study. Jeff did his thing . . . he organized a prayer vigil for me. The next morning the police contacted my parents, the last people who were known to have seen me before my disappearance. They told the police that I was perfectly safe, but that I had gone out of town to think things over because I was having doubts about my forthcoming marriage. The police bought that. After all, why would my parents lie about such a thing?

Christine remembered insisting to the police that she suspected foul play. They hadn't been too sympathetic, but did agree to question my parents again. After a second and a third interrogation, my parents became rather hostile to the police. They complained that they were being harassed and the police had no right to concern themselves with a family affair. The police backed off. Frustrated by this turn of events, Christine and Jeff told everything to a Boston newspaper in hopes of stirring up some official investigation and action. The paper interviewed them for four hours, but held back on printing the story until they could verify it.

She also remembered the ugly crank call on Friday, a voice shouting the Jewish Defense League slogan, "Never again!" Then silence.

She remembered the painful duty of informing close friends and relatives that the wedding was postponed. She recalled the anguish of the wedding day itself, the second crank call she received an hour after the wedding time, the voice that mocked her: "Weren't you to have been married today? What happened to your friend? Too bad he didn't show up!"

She remembered the sleepless nights, the worry, the nagging fear that she, too, might be kidnapped, the kindness and prayers of concerned friends. Now the waiting was over, and soon we would be together.

She pushed down on the gas pedal and drove the old car as fast as she dared. She was almost there, when suddenly, outside of Newburgh, New York, the car sputtered and came to a gradual stop. She steered over to the side of the road before the engine died. Nothing she did would start it again. She had to have a passerby telephone for a tow truck, and they took more than an hour to get to her. When Chris finally got the car to a garage, she found it had a broken fuel pump. She left the car there to be fixed, and frantically called the Newburgh police.

After she explained her emergency and her need to get to me in a hurry, the Newburgh police came for her in a patrol car. They couldn't take her all the way into Middletown, because it wasn't their territory. But they drove her to the edge of town, and from there the Middletown police took her the rest of the way. What a strange reunion awaited us at that Middletown police station.

Chapter 13

If I Made it Up, Why Am I Here?

The wheels of justice turn very slowly. When the first officer picked me up at Wurtsboro, it was only about 6:30 a.m. Once he satisfied himself that I wasn't a criminal, he began to question me about the details of my confinement and escape. I guess he felt sorry for me because I looked like I was in pretty bad shape, and he bought me a cup of coffee. It felt so good to be sitting in a restaurant. For a while I had given up all hope of ever seeing the inside of a public eating place again because the deprogrammers had almost convinced me my only choice was to live in accordance with the strictest orthodox Judaism for the rest of my life. For the first time since my capture I was doing something natural to my lifestyle. After the coffee, we got to the Wurtsboro station and had to wait for the investigator, Inspector Mason. He was the one who called Christine later to verify my story.

When Mason came, he questioned me for a long time. After I finished telling him what happened, he leaned toward me with a stern look.

"Listen," he warned, "if you're lying, you're going to be in an awful lot of trouble. You've just told me a story of conspiracy. It's a federal offense in the three states you're talking about, and it sounds like there are twenty or thirty people who could go to jail. If you're just trying to get home, or you're making up a story to get your name in the paper, you'd better tell me right now. Lying is only a misdemeanor. We'd fine you right now and send you out of here, or give you a short sentence, but at least the thing wouldn't go any further than you and it wouldn't involve other people. You're opening yourself up to law suits and everything, accusing people."

"I'm telling you the truth!"

"You say your father did this all because he didn't want you to marry a Christian girl?"

"That's right," I told him.

Mason fixed me with another fish-eyed stare. "Would you be willing to take a lie detector test?"

"Sure, I'll take one if you want me to," I said.

"Would you like to call your father?" I could tell he still wasn't believing me.

"Sure." I gave him my parents' Newton phone number. They put the call through and the officer and inspector both listened on extension phones.

My mother answered the phone. "Kennie!" she screamed hysterically, "are you O.K.?"

"Yeah, I'm O.K.," I answered her.

She was crying and saying she loved me and asking over and over if I was sure that I was O.K., and I kept telling her that I was fine.

"We've been sitting in this house for two weeks, praying for you. The whole family has been doing nothing else the whole time! Are you sure you're O.K.?" I felt for the first time in two years she was being totally open with me. The deprogrammers had told me that my parents didn't know where I was or exactly what was happening to me. I hadn't believed them then, but now hearing how upset my mother was, I could believe it. Evidently, once the deprogrammers had me, they didn't want the family involved with any of the details. Maybe my mother regretted taking such drastic action. At least she sounded sincerely worried.

"Where are you? Who's with you?"

"I'm with friends, now," I told her. The police had instructed me not to give away where I was.

"Are you with the organization?"

"What organization?" I asked. I couldn't tell if she meant Jews for Jesus or the deprogrammers.

"The organization!" she repeated without explaining.

"No, I'm with friends, but I can't tell you right now where I am."

"Can I come and see you?" she asked.

"I don't know," I told her. "I'll have to see about that . . . Have you been in touch with Chris?"

"Yes," she said. "She's O.K., don't worry."

Then my younger brother David got on the phone. "Are you still Kennie?" he asked.

"Yeah, of course. I'm still the same person." I wondered what my parents had said to him.

He sensed the strain of the situation and tried to find a point of normalcy. "When are we going camping?"

"First chance we get," I promised.

I asked if my father was home, and my mother said he was out right then. He wasn't at work, either, but would call me back soon. I gave her the number of the station without telling her it was police headquarters. Then I sat there, talking to the police officers until about thirty minutes later, the telephone rang, and they had me answer it.

"Hello, Ken?" My father sounded happy to hear from me. "I'm glad to know that you're safe. I just wanted you to know the truth before I die. I just wanted you to see the other side."

He started reminiscing on the phone about my childhood and how much he loved me, and the time he saved me from drowning.

"What do you mean before you die?" I interrupted.

"I just found out I have cancer," he told me. I was shocked and upset. Confused and exhausted as I was, I started to apologize to him for the things I had done to let him down, imaginary and real. At this writing, I still don't know if he was telling me the truth about his physical condition.

"I'd like to see you," he went on. "Can we arrange a meeting? Get together and talk?"

"Sure," I told him. "I'd like to talk to you."

"Are you alone now? Who are you with . . . ?"

Before I could answer, one of the officers held out a scrawled note to me: ASK HIM WHY HE HAD YOU KIDNAPPED.

"Dad," I broke in, "why did you have me kidnapped?"

"I didn't have you kidnapped!"

"What do you mean, you didn't have me kidnapped?" I was amazed that he could say that. "You were right there when it happened. Don't you remember?"

The more I protested that I had been kidnapped, the

more he kept repeating, "I didn't have you kidnapped!" Then his manner changed. "Now, Ken," he chided me, "you know you're in a prolonged state of adolescence, you have emotional problems, a lot of things on your mind. I think you should rest and we should talk. Can we meet some place? Is anybody listening to this phone conversation?"

At that point, Investigator Mason informed him he was listening. "Mr. Levitt, this is Investigator Mason from the New York State Police. We have your son here. He just told us that he was kidnapped from your home and held captive in two different places and he finally escaped."

By now I was really upset. "What're you talking about, Dad?" I continued. "How can you say all that? If I made the whole thing up, then what am I doing all the way down here?"

He wouldn't discuss what had happened, but kept insisting that we meet somewhere and talk. I thought maybe I'd better arrange to meet him so I could get the whole mess straightened out. I figured he was afraid to admit anything over the phone with the police listening.

"O.K., I'll try to work something out and call you back," I promised. The police were signalling me to end the conversation, so I told him good-bye and hung up.

The investigator sent me with another officer to get some breakfast in the restaurant next door. I was so tired and upset about the conversation with my father that I couldn't eat, or talk very coherently to this new officer. I must have really seemed like a mental case to him. I was so tired, my mind was drifting, and I could hardly pay attention to our conversation.

He looked at me too gently over his coffee cup. "Ever see a psychiatrist?" he asked.

I said yes, I had, in high school.

"Well," he tried to sound comforting. "It's not bad to see a psychiatrist. A lot of people do who aren't necessarily crazy."

I thought, "Why's he talking to me like this? This guy really believes that I'm sick. He believes I made up the whole story." By then I was too tired to care if he believed me or not. I had hardly slept, and I was shivering because I had run through some fields in my escape and my clothes were wet with dew and perspiration. As wild, dirty, and unkempt as I looked, I can't blame him for questioning my sanity.

When we went back inside the police station, Investigator Mason had some good news for me.

"Well, Ken," he reported. "We called Christine and she confirmed your story. She's on her way up here. Come along with us in the car, and we'll just check this thing out."

We got back in the patrol car and retraced the whole path of my escape from Camp Emunah. They questioned me as we rode about my father and the importance he attached to my being his firstborn son and not following the religion of my childhood. I explained as best I could about the religious role of the firstborn in Judaism.

"By the way," Mason asked, "what did your mother mean by 'the organization'?"

"I'm not really sure," I told him. "She could have meant the people who had me, or maybe she meant the group I was associated with in Boston, Jews for Jesus."

When I mentioned Jews who believed in Jesus the police got more confused and incredulous than ever. A Jew who believes in Jesus is kidnapped by his own father and confined with orthodox Jews who try to get him not to believe? To them, it sounded like a cheap drugstore novel or the ravings of a lunatic.

Investigator Mason warned me again, "If you're lying . . . we told you what the problem was. Are you *sure* this all happened?

"I'm not lying, I told you before!" I was really getting tired of not being believed.

"Well, all right, and you're willing to take a polygraph test?" I guess he still wasn't convinced.

As we reached the campgrounds in the police car, Frank Leavitt and the deprogrammers were clustered together outside, talking. I think they were trying to formulate some plan of action after discovering my escape. I'm sure they weren't altogether surprised to see me show up with the police.

Shmuel walked cautiously over to me. "Chayim! You

should'a woke me if you had something you wanted to talk about. You didn't have to run away." His tone was nervous and condescending, as though he were reprimanding a naughty child.

I didn't say anything. They must have decided that it would be foolish to deny that I had been there, but obviously they weren't going to acknowledge that I had been held against my will.

The officer approached Frank. He gestured toward me, "Mr. Leavitt, he claims he was being held captive here and ran away."

Frank denied that he knew anything about my being held at Camp Emunah against my will. I had told the officers back at the police station that he might not realize the full implications of the situation. Still, it seemed rather odd that he would see that I was being guarded and not question why. What, if anything, had the deprogrammers told him about me? I couldn't be sure about how involved he was, but I felt sorry for him. He hadn't treated me badly like the others had in Long Island. I was really glad that those others were on hand to see the police come, especially Shmuel. He had been so smug about my never getting away, about it being God's will that I should return to orthodox Judaism. I hoped that now maybe my escape would show them all that God wanted it my way, not theirs. Then, too, it wasn't right that they should all go scot-free to do the same thing to other innocent victims like me. It wasn't a matter of being vindictive, but rather of protecting the future religious rights of others.

The state trooper asked me if I could confirm that I had really been at Camp Emunah. Had I left anything behind in the bunk? I remembered I had accidentally left my sweater there.

He went into the cabin and came back holding my grey pullover sweater, and a skull cap.

"I found these stuffed into a pillowcase," he said. "Are they yours?"

I told him that they were mine, and that corroborated my story. Then he took another look around and wrote a few things in a notebook he carried.

On leaving he warned Frank, "Mr. Leavitt, you'd better stick around. Police and investigators will be here later and they'll want to talk to you."

Frank looked uncomfortable. "I'll be contacting my lawyer, but it's Friday, almost time for my sabbath. I don't take care of any business on the sabbath."

The two officers and I got back into the police car, heading this time for Ellenville. Mason shook his head.

"It's incredible. A soap opera! I can't believe it!"

The other officer agreed. "Me neither, but I'm beginning to!"

Chapter 14
Wheels of Justice

The Ellenville police station was no bigger than the Wurtsboro station. They both looked like old residence buildings that had been done over, producing at least a semi-official effect. As we came in I saw several state policemen in full uniform busying themselves with the routine tasks of the day. Someone showed me upstairs to a small private office, where I sat by myself while Mason and the other officer explained my story downstairs.

I tried to clean up a bit in the washroom, and waited, shivering again in the cold air from the air conditioner because my clothes were still damp. A blonde plainclothesman kept wandering in and out of the office as I sat there. He had his coat off, and I could plainly see the gun and holster strapped to his waist. That made him look very official and somewhat intimidating.

Every time he came in, ostensibly to get some file or paper from the desk, he'd ask me a question or two in passing. He'd say things to impress me with the seriousness of the crime I was reporting, and most of the time he acted like he didn't believe me. This added to my tension and uneasiness.

After a while, another fellow came in. He, too, was in plain clothes, but I felt less threatened by him. He was smiling.

"Are you cold?" He turned down the air conditioner.

"Well, you say this all happened because your parents didn't want you to marry a girl of a different religion? Unbelievable!"

I nodded.

"I can relate to that," he went on. "When I was getting married, we had a big hassle, too. My wife is Protestant and I'm Catholic. When you get married, you should move far away from your parents ... Now, I'm going to ask you some questions. It's going to take a while, but just be patient. I want you to remember as best you possibly can every single detail."

He sat down at a typewriter and started to record all my answers to his questions.

"I'm going to have you read this and sign it when I'm finished," he explained. "If you see anything that's wrong, I want you to bring it to my attention, and we'll change it."

By the time he finished asking me everything, almost an hour and a half more had passed. The document ended up being four pages long, and I had to read it very carefully before signing the original and two copies. He changed the places I indicated weren't right, and then I initialled each change.

While I was giving this officer my official statement, my parents called again. They both sounded very upset, and begged me to reconsider giving my statement to the police.

"Ken, what's going on there? You're making a big mistake! A lot of people are going to be in unnecessary trouble. You're getting too involved, and you don't know what you're doing. You're very tired. It's all a misunderstanding, a family matter, and we can take care of this whole thing. Can't we get together and talk? We'll drive up and meet you there."

They kept insisting that I was irrational and that I had made up the whole thing. I knew it had happened, and it just blew my mind that they were trying to deny it.

"I don't know if I can meet you. I don't want to get kidnapped again," I told them.

My mother's entire attitude and manner changed. No longer open and solicitous, she sided angrily with my father. "You weren't kidnapped! No one's going to kidnap you."

I felt badly that they were both so upset, but I had to go through with it.

"Look," I said, "I have to get to the bottom of this. Chris is coming up, and I'll let you know later, after she comes, what I'm going to do."

I really intended to call them back and try to straighten things out, but as it happened, I got too involved and didn't have time to call them until several days later.

The blonde detective with the gun and holster had come

back in and was listening in and talking to my parents, too. After I got off the phone, I could hear his end of the conversation as he talked with them. My father was telling him that I was not emotionally well and had made the whole thing up. The detective stared at me over the receiver as he talked with them.

"Yes, I see . . . Uhuh, yes, that's possible . . . We could get an examination . . . yes."

I felt panic welling up inside me. What if they got a doctor to examine me and somehow got him to say I was incompetent? They would force me to go back to my parents, who might turn me over to the deprogrammers again. I knew I was rational and in control, but if they could convince the doctor that I had made up the kidnap story, that would easily prove to him that I was insane. A person would *have* to be sick to make up a story like that!

The detective got off the phone and came over to me. "Your parents tell me this didn't really happen, that you made the whole thing up." He sounded annoyed that I had put the whole police staff to so much trouble.

I protested again that I was telling the truth.

"Well, just wait here," he said.

Another detective came in with a message for me from the Boston Jews for Jesus office: "Call Moishe Rosen in San Francisco." While I was trying to sort out my thoughts about my parents and thinking about calling San Francisco, Detective Mahoney walked in. He was round faced, of medium build, and had a pleasant manner; but there was an air of businesslike efficiency about him.

"O.K., what's the story here? Let's get to the bottom of this." He sat me down, impatient to finish the matter.

"So what're we going to do now? We've got this description. You've been kidnapped, we've gotcha out of there, we have your statement, what do we do now? Do you want to go ahead with this and press charges?"

I hesitated. "I don't know. I don't think so."

"What do you mean," he exploded. "After all this you're not going to press charges? I suggest that you do press charges, not for your sake, but for the sake of anybody who's involved with these people. Who knows how many others they had locked up in that place before you? We can't have people going around dragging others off the streets and holding them captive!"

The blonde detective had finally decided that I was telling the truth, and he chimed in, too, urging me to press charges.

When I still hesitated, Mahoney really got angry. He slammed his fist down on the desk. "O.K., don't press charges! But next time they get you, don't come to us!"

Then they laid a guilt trip on me about bothering the police and taking up so much time, then not following through.

"Is this story true, or isn't it? Were you being held at Camp Emunah, or not? Could you have left at any time? What happened when you called Christine from there? Didn't they listen in on your conversation and give you only a limited time to talk? You call that freedom? You were being held there, being held captive. There's no doubt about it, you should press charges!"

I realized they were right, but still I hesitated. I hated making trouble.

"Just a minute," I said. "Can I call someone?"

Mahoney oozed impatience. "What difference is that going to make?"

"Well," I told him, "he knows a lot about this kind of situation. He's dealt with problems like this before."

"Who is this guy, anyhow?"

I told them Moishe Rosen was the leader of Jews for Jesus, an organization of Jewish people who believe Jesus is the Messiah. As usual, with most people, this explanation produced puzzled looks from Mahoney and the blonde detective.

Mahoney just wanted to get on with it. He cut short my involved description.

"Yeah, go ahead and call this guy."

"I'll just talk a minute or so," I promised.

"It's all right, talk as long as you want, you're not kidnapped any more. Take your time."

I put through the call to Moishe. Mahoney sat there, shuffling papers on his desk, looking up to listen every so often. Moishe advised me to go through with the charges, and I was saying, "O.K. . . . yeah, I will . . . ." At that, Mahoney perked up and looked relieved. I let him talk to Moishe.

"Yeah, right! I agree." Mahoney nodded his head vigorously. "Absolutely! . . . Definitely! Yeah, who knows how many others they had up there! . . . Yeah, right. I told him that! O.K., thanks. A pleasure!" He hung up and turned to me.

"We'll get this thing typed up now."

I still felt bad. "Are you going to arrest Frank Leavitt? Can't we just press charges on the kidnappers?"

Mahoney shook his head. "It can't be done that way. In order to get the kidnappers, we have to start from the end and work back. You can drop the charges any time you want after we get it rolling."

They made out a complaint against Frank and the blonde detective took me over to the courthouse to talk to the judge. The courthouse looked like something out of a movie. It was in the back of some kind of a municipal garage or public works department. The place was full of police equipment. There was a motorcycle parked in the room next to the judge's office, and a motorcycle helmet was lying on his desk. They introduced me to the judge, who shook my hand. He was dressed in casual clothes, no robe, and I think I was his only case for the day.

By the time I finished with the judge, it was midafternoon. Then the officer who had taken down my statement drove me and another policeman in an unmarked car back to Camp Emunah. They were going to arrest Frank, and I had to go along to make the identification. I hated doing that.

"Are you really going to arrest him?" I asked Mahoney. "He's concerned about being home for the sabbath."

"Don't worry," he assured me. "All we'll do is bring him down here, fingerprint him, take a picture, get bail posted, and he'll be free to leave. Lots of Jewish people live around here, and I know about things like sabbath keeping. We won't keep him too long."

The camp looked deserted when we pulled up. I stayed in the back of the car, and the two officers went up to Frank's house. His wife, wearing the familiar green bandana, opened the door.

"I'm sorry," I heard her say. "I can't really talk to you right now. I'm getting ready for the sabbath. You'll have to come back on Sunday. Frank isn't here right now, and everyone else is gone. I can't really do anything. Please don't make any noise because the baby is sleeping."

It sounded to me like she was stalling, and the officers thought so, too. I could tell by the look they exchanged, as if to say, "Oh, well, that's a typical reaction. They do it every time."

"Well, ma'am," one of them asked, "is it all right if we just wait for him to come back?"

"We're not going to answer any questions without our lawyer!" she said. Obviously someone had already advised them on how to act if the police came back.

The two officers told her they would just wait for Frank.

"He won't be back for quite a while," she insisted. "And when he does get back, he's got a lot of things to do before the sabbath, and he won't have time to talk to you." She was really out to protect her husband.

The officers were not to be put off. "We'll wait," they told her, and went back to the car.

While we waited for Frank to come back, we talked. I told them about the deprogrammers' telling me there was a declaration of incompetence out on me that would force me to stay in their custody.

"Man," they said, "that's incredible. We can see that you obviously are competent. We have to get to the bottom of this thing."

After a while, we saw Frank's big black pickup truck coming down the road. As he got out of the truck, the police showed him the warrant.

"Can we ask you some questions?"

"Sure." He looked worried.

"Can you come along now?"

Frank looked more upset. "I already told them that I couldn't be available until Sunday because of the sabbath, because of my religion."

The police politely insisted. "Unfortunately the federal law does not take that into consideration. This is the only possible time we can take you. It'll have to be now."

Frank sighed resignedly. "I don't travel on the sabbath. May I just go inside and get a few religious objects in case it takes too long and I don't get back in time?"

The police waited while Frank ran into the house. He came back a few minutes later carrying his prayer shawl and phylacteries, a jacket, and two loaves of *chalah*, special sabbath bread. Without a word, he got into the back seat with me. I could see he was quite upset and trying to act nonchalant. Obviously he was prepared to be detained for quite a while. Those loaves of sabbath bread would be his only food until Saturday night if he didn't get back home before sundown. He wouldn't eat anything the police provided because it wasn't kosher.

I admired his dedication, and I really felt bad for him. "Sorry, Frank," I offered. "This was the only way we could get the people who kidnapped me." He gave me a reproachful stare and didn't answer.

One of the officers turned around from the front seat and warned, "You're not supposed to talk to each other. That's federal law."

I shrugged my assent. I figured Frank didn't really want to talk to me anyhow. I had the feeling that he thought I was anti-Semitic and was enjoying ruining his sabbath. I wished I didn't have to cause him any trouble, but I would have had a hard time getting him to believe that.

Chapter 15

Go West, Young Man

When I got back to Ellenville with the two officers and Frank Leavitt, Steve Cohen from the New York City Jews for Jesus office was waiting for me. Moishe Rosen had told me earlier over the telephone that Steve was coming up right away to help me. Before talking to Moishe, I thought I was very much alone in that whole terrible situation, but as we talked I began to realize that I had a family of fellow believers who were rallying around me. I found out that people all over the country had been praying for me ever since my disappearance. There were many who were waiting to help me, and I was very definitely not alone.

Steve had instructions to stay with me all the way. He was to help me deal with the police and get me reunited with Christine. Then he was to help make all necessary arrangements for the two of us to get to another part of the country for safety's sake. Moishe had asked me over the telephone to decide if I would rather go to Chicago or San Francisco for a while. Both cities had Jews for Jesus personnel who could help me, and both were far away from the East Coast and the deprogrammers.

While I was at the courthouse talking to the judge and at Camp Emunah during Frank's arrest, Steve was already in Ellenville, making arrangements and taking care of details. Now that I was back at the police station, he hung in with me every minute, hovering over me like a mother hen.

"Don't worry, Ken," he assured me. "I'll take care of everything from here on. I'm going to stick with you every minute."

I appreciated his calm efficiency. It was great to have someone else take over, to know that I was safe and had friends who really cared.

Steve made sure the police realized the seriousness of

the whole situation and my potential danger. The people who had captured me now had good reasons for preventing me from testifying against them, and they might try to kidnap me again. Steve arranged security measures with the police to insure my safety.

During the time I was at the Ellenville police station, a Lieutenant Cox called from Boston. I thought he might have been contacted by Jeff Fritz, who was also working on helping me. Cox wanted to know if I was coming back to Massachusetts, and if so, did I want police protection? They would provide a police escort if Christine and I would be driving back to Boston.

"I don't know," I told him. "I'm not sure if or when I'm coming back to Boston. I'll get back to you on that."

It was getting late now, about four or five o'clock in the afternoon, and we began to worry that Christine hadn't arrived yet. At first, I thought the police were bringing her up from Boston. It seemed logical to me that if they wanted to talk to her, they would make arrangements to get her there. When I found out that she was driving up by herself, I worried for her safety. She had started out early enough to have gotten there by now, and I started to wonder if maybe she, too, could have been kidnapped. I could see the deprogrammers tailing her all the way from Boston just to find me, or grabbing her to bait me into revealing my whereabouts. Even Mahoney was getting worried. He checked and found out that Christine was coming to Middletown, about forty-five minutes away, rather than Ellenville. Then, after what seemed like hours more, Mahoney got a message from the Middletown station that Christine had finally arrived.

I couldn't wait to get over to Middletown. Hastily, I arranged to keep in touch with the Ellenville police if they needed me for any more information. Then Steve and I got into his van, heading for Middletown and my reunion with Chris.

By then I was faint with hunger because I hadn't eaten anything since dinner time the previous day. I had been too upset to touch the breakfast the policeman offered me when

I first escaped. Steve stopped to get some fast takeout food at a hamburger place.

"Lock yourself inside the car while I'm in there," he instructed me.

I followed his suggestion, marvelling at the high level of security he felt was necessary. Still, the more I thought about it, the more I could see that he was right. After my successful escape I thought I was no longer in any serious danger, but the longer I was free, and looking back at the situation objectively, the more I sensed the intensity of purpose that those deprogrammers had, and it scared me.

We finally arrived at Middletown about six o'clock. The police station there was much bigger than either Ellenville or Wurtsboro. They had a modern, official-looking building, and a big parking lot. As we pulled up and parked, I saw Christiane running out to meet us. She had been anxiously watching through the window. It was so good to see her. She hugged me, filthy and disheveled as I was. I'm sure she must have been shocked at my terrible appearance, but she acted normally. We went inside, and Steve left us alone for a few minutes while he went to make some phone calls.

As we were talking, suddenly Steve reappeared and shouted across the room.

"Hey, where would you like to go—San Francisco or Chicago?"

I looked at him like he had just dropped in from Mars. "San Francisco or Chicago? What do you mean?" I had forgotten about my conversation with Moishe earlier.

"You're leaving tonight," Steve informed me. "Where do you want to go?"

I looked questioningly at Chris. "What would you like?"

She was caught unprepared, too. She looked at me, round-eyed. "I don't know!" Neither of us is prone to making snap decisions, especially about big important matters. Beside that, I found out later that at that point Chris wasn't quite sure that I still wanted to marry her, and she was worried about being stranded clear across the country.

I asked Steve what he thought about it. "Moishe thinks

that San Francisco would be better than Chicago, but it's really up to you," he said.

"O.K.," I decided. "We'll go to San Francisco. Yeah, San Francisco sounds good!

Steve went back to his telephoning. He got us two reservations on the night flight from Kennedy airport. It would arrive in San Francisco at 2:00 a.m. Pacific Daylight Time.

All our belongings that Chris had packed in Boston were still in Greg's car. We drove over to the garage where Christine had left the car to be fixed. She arranged for the garage to contact Greg about the repairs, and then we transferred our luggage to Steve's van. It was a very strange assortment. There was Christine's suitcase and the garment bag with her long white dress and my good suit. But Chris hadn't been able to fit all my clothes into her suitcase, so she had stuffed some of my things into brown paper shopping bags. The paper shopping bags added the last bizarre touch to my weird appearance. I was still dirty and scraggly, with a heavy beard and wild-looking hair. I wore a rope around my waist instead of a belt. I wondered what the people at the airport check-in would think. But then, I thought, one often sees strange looking people in airports!

On our way to the airport, I call Jeff Fritz in Boston and I asked him to inform Lieutenant Cox that I wouldn't be needing police protection in Boston for a while. Jeff was really into the cloak-and-dagger frame of mind. He kept the conversation very tense, cautioning me not to disclose anything important as we talked, in case his phone was bugged.

"O.K., Ken, I'll take care of things. We love you and Chris . . . we're praying for you. 'Bye now." He hung up.

By this time we had to move quickly in order not to miss our 10:30 flight. When we went through the security area, I'm sure they must have double checked those shopping bags when they caught sight of me. But at last Chris and I were safely seated on the plane, and on our way to California.

I took a heady, almost childlike delight in flying, and kept trying to see out of the window. As the huge engines strained and we lifted off the ground with a mighty burst of power, I felt really free at last. It was such a relief!

I kept repeating, "I can't believe it! I can't believe I really got away from there!"

Even though we were both exhausted, we couldn't sleep. We didn't get the chance to talk much though. I'd been told by Steve that I should write everything I could remember about my ordeal while it was still fresh in my mind, and that took most of the five hours of flying time.

Sooner than we anticipated, the captain announced our arrival in San Francisco. As I peered out of the window at the twinkling lights and watched the ground come up to meet us, it was all like a dream. I had always wanted to see California, but not quite like this!

When we stumbled bleary-eyed into the terminal, three Jews for Jesus staff members were waiting to welcome us. I recognized Susan Perlman, information officer in charge of media. The others were new to me—tall, curly-haired and beared Jim Warnock and his wife, Kresha. I don't know exactly why Moishe chose them to pick us up. Maybe it was because Jim had experience in the armed forces and was brawny enough to fend off any potential physical assault, or maybe it was because Jim is Moishe's secretary and right-hand man. Certainly doe-eyed, pug-nosed Susan and pert, five-foot-two pink-cheeked Kresha wouldn't lend much muscle to a dangerous situation. On the other hand, they're both pros at public speaking and could scream loudly and shrilly if necessary. That, in a public place, would be enough to stop any kidnappers dead in their tracks.

We couldn't be sure that no one had followed us, or was looking for us when we landed. Susan was in charge. She thought it best that we split up until we were safely out of the airport. She took me and Kresha to her car while Jim and Christine waited for the luggage. Jim was keeping a close watch on Chris in the crowded baggage area. He had a momentary scare when a woman elbowed her way between him and Chris and they were temporarily separated, but it turned out that the woman was no kidnapper, just an impatient suitcase owner trying to retrieve her baggage.

At last they got the luggage and we were safely in the car.

As we rode along, Susan mentioned the possibility of our getting married the next day if we wanted to.

"There's a three day wait for a license in California," she explained, "but if you go up to Nevada, you can get married right away. Reno's not too far from San Francisco."

"Reno?" I thought. That was a place I only knew from the movies and television, a storybook land full of cowboys, actors, and gamblers. Everything seemed so far removed from reality, and Chris and I were too tired to think or make plans. We had to get some rest.

Susan dropped me and Jim and Kresha at their apartment, then took Christine home with her. By then it was about three o'clock San Francisco time and six in the morning for Chris and me, because physically we were still on Eastern time. I showered and lay down on the bed Kresha fixed up for me, but it was a long time before I could fall asleep. Even then, I didn't sleep more than three or four hours.

The next day when I talked to Christine, she told me she had only slept one hour herself. In strange surroundings, frustrated about not getting to talk to me very much, she was awake most of the night worrying that I might get kidnapped again before we could see each other in the morning.

Saturday morning I got my first look at San Francisco in the daylight. Jim drove me to Jews for Jesus headquarters, and I found myself sitting in Moishe Rosen's offices.

Moishe is a tall, heavyset fellow. His soft spoken voice and slow, gentle manner sharply contrast that huge frame, and his cheeks dimple when he smiles. He smiled his Chevrolet grille smile under a salt and pepper mustache.

"Well, Ken, how're you feeling?"

We talked for a while. "Do you feel confused about some of the questions the deprogrammers raised?" Moishe asked.

I nodded. "I still believe in Jesus, but they did bring up some confusing points about certain verses."

Patiently Moishe got out a Bible concordance and talked to me about some of the things that were troubling me. We looked up many verses and discussed them until I felt more confident. He also helped me to see the whole ordeal in proper perspective and to understand the tactics the deprogrammers had used on me.

"These people, or a similar group, have done this same thing to others," he told me. "We have a tape recording of another young man's story that is very similar to the account you've given us." He said I could hear it later.

"How's your spiritual life?" he asked me. "Have you been able to read the Bible and pray yet?"

I told him I had been reading the Bible just that morning at Jim's house, and that God was still real to me.

Then Moishe called Christine into the office, too. We sat and talked for a couple of hours. Then he looked at Chris with a twinkle in his eye.

"You still want to marry this guy?"

Chris nodded and smiled.

"Ken, you want to get married?"

"Yes. Sure I want to get married!"

Moishe called Jim into the office. "Drive these two up to Reno and let's get them married. They've waited long enough!"

Chapter 16

New Ties, Old Ties

"But thou, O LORD, art a shield for me; my glory, and the lifter up of mine head.

I cried unto the LORD with my voice, and he heard me out of his holy hill. Selah.

I laid me down and slept; I awakened; for the LORD sustained me. (Psalm 3:3-5)

June 3, 1978—our wedding day! It was almost two weeks later than planned, and not at all the way Christine and I had imagined it. We zipped along the superhighway between San Francisco and Reno that sunny Saturday afternoon in the big brown and yellow Dodge maxi-van. People in cars around us occasionally honked a greeting and made a ONE WAY hand sign as they noticed the two-foot tall JEWS FOR JESUS decals painted on both sides of the van. A few others, obviously not believers, reacted with less complimentary gestures as they whizzed by. Jim, our driver, didn't bat an eyelash. The lanky, ex-Coast Guard man was cool mannered about everything, including hastily arranged marriages. Besides, he was quite accustomed to driving one of these fifty-five mile-an-hour moving billboards, and to the accompanying responses, good and bad.

Also in the van with us rode Jim's wife, Kresha and Mary Kaye, another Jews for Jesus staffer we had just met. We had only known these people a few hours, but now they were about to play some very important roles in our lives. They were sharing a day with us that we would always remember. They would be our wedding attendants, our witnesses, our only guests, and our only family present, related not by blood ties, but by our common bond in Christ.

The quick civil ceremony we were going to have would contrast sharply with the joyful, serene occasion we had looked forward to for so long. We would miss having our

New England friends and family share this special time with us. Still, and most important, there *would* be a wedding.

The bizzare adventure that had spoiled our carefully made wedding plans was over, but the ordeal, less than forty-eight hours in the past, lingered vividly in my thoughts as we rode along. Muscles still protesting from my nightmarish confinement and dash for freedom, eyes gritty from lack of sleep, part of me refused to believe it had all really happened.

Held prisoner for two weeks by the deprogrammers, I couldn't rid myself of the jarring memories. Their voices still rang in my ears.

"Murderer! Nazi! Your hands drip with the blood of six million of our Jewish people! You deserve to suffer like they did in the concentration camps and gas chambers. We're going to give you a taste of your own medicine!"

I wasn't an anti-Semite. I hadn't killed anyone, or wished anyone harm. How could they accuse me of such things simply because I believed that Jesus Christ was the promised Messiah of Israel? How could they take upon themselves the role of judge, jury, and yes, even executioner in a sense? I didn't quite know. But two things I did know beyond doubt: despite their attempts to kill my two most sacred commitments, I had won the battle. I still loved Jesus, and He hadn't stopped being my Lord and Savior; I still loved Christine, she still loved me, and despite our ruined wedding plans, today we would become man and wife. My zealous but misguided captors had tried to rob me of both of these things, and my sanity as well. But by God's grace, they had failed.

The trip from San Francisco to Reno takes about five hours, time enough to relax and enjoy the grandeur of the High Sierra scenery. But Chris and I were too exhausted and too keyed up to notice much. In the back seat of the van I squeezed Christine's hand reassuringly. She smiled at me. It was good just to look at her after so recently wondering when, if ever, I would see her again. Her pretty face looked pale, and I noticed shadowed circles under her eyes. How she must have suffered. I wasn't the only one who had just endured a terrible ordeal.

"We're almost there, Chris," I whispered.

She nodded and smiled again. "I know."

Several miles from our destination we started seeing billboards everywhere. The roadside was peppered with signs
advertising restaurants, gambling casinos, and quick wedding chapels. One sign read, "Chapel of Promise—24 Hour
Service." We jotted down the highway directions as we drove
past.

Knowing beforehand that Reno was a gaudy gambling
town didn't fully prepare us for the shock of seeing it. We
tried to adjust as Jim parked the van and we entered the re-
ceptionist's area of the Chapel of Promise. Covered with
flocked paper reminiscent of a ladies' powder room, the
walls boasted pictures of happy, smiling customers. The
room's decor was punctuated here and there by arrangements of flowers guaranteed never to wilt—because they
were plastic. Behind a desk sat a plump, motherly looking
woman.

"Could we have a religious ceremony?" we asked.

"Sorry," she smiled. "We have a standard service ap-
proved by Nevada law. You can stay in the chapel a few minutes longer afterwards if you want to do something religious
on your own."

She wrote down a time slot for our ceremony and sent
us off to get the marriage license. Our Massachusetts license,
even if we had had it with us, would not have been valid in
Nevada. The wedding chapel provided a special shuttle car
just for the purpose of bringing couples back and forth between the chapel and the license bureau. The teenaged boy
who drove the car also doubled as photographer. Slight of
build, he either looked very young for his age, or he was driving without a driver's license. He looked as though he were
enjoying his job as he bustled around importantly. Back at
the Chapel of Promise, we had to wait our turn. We changed
into our wedding clothes in a dressing room just as garish as
the rest of the place, and wondered if the chapel itself
matched the rest of the decor. At last they called our names.
They showed us into a tiny room, bare except for three or

four hard pews and a wooden pulpit backed by some curtains.

"Stand right there," directed our young chauffeur-photographer.

As we took our places, a short, stocky "minister" appeared from somewhere behind the curtains. He was as impeccably dressed as a funeral director, but his face was frozen into a professionally happy wedding smile. He fixed us with a bespectacled gaze and with hardly any preliminaries, began the ceremony. While he spoke, the kid scurried about, snapping pictures, popping flash bulbs in our faces. In five minutes, it was over, and the "minister" disappeared behind the curtains as quickly and silently as he had come in.

The photographer took a few more pictures and left, too. Christine and I looked at each other. We didn't feel really married yet.

"Let's pray," someone said.

We bowed our heads and our new friends prayed God's blessings on our marriage.

"Lord, You know Ken and Chris wanted a different kind of wedding ceremony, one that would be a testimony and honor You. But You also know why that wasn't possible. We pray that You will honor the intentions of our hearts. Thank You for bringing Ken safely out of his ordeal. Now, please bless this service and their new life together. In Jesus' Name, amen."

Jim opened the Bible we had brought and began to read.

"And I will put enmity between thee and the woman. . . ."

More than a little startled, I raised an eyebrow at him. He blithely went on reading.

". . . unto the woman he said, I will multiply thy sorrows . . ." As if we hadn't had enough sorrows recently!

Jim plowed on. When he got to, "Cursed is the ground for thy sake," I couldn't stand it any more. I had to interrupt.

"Jim, those have to be the wrong verses!"

He looked up from the Bible. "Yeah," he mused. "I thought those didn't sounds right!"

Our puzzlement turned to laughter as we figured out that

we had told him to read the wrong chapter of Genesis. After the tension and rush of the past days and hours, it provided a welcome moment of relief. Then undaunted and cool as ever, our pinch-hit preacher found the right place and read:

> And the Lord God said, It is not good that the man should be alone; I will make him an help meet for him ... And the Lord God caused a deep sleep to fall upon Adam, and he slept; and he took one of his ribs, and closed up the flesh instead thereof;

> And the rib, which the Lord God had taken from man, made he a woman, and brought her unto the man.

> And Adam said, This is now bone of my bones, and flesh of my flesh; she shall be called Woman, because she was taken out of Man.

> Therefore shall a man leave his father and his mother, and shall cleave unto his wife: and they shall be one flesh.

We smiled our relief and agreement. That was certainly much better.

Jim continued reading from Proverbs 3:1-10, finishing with verses Christine and I had chosen from I John 4. At the close of the prayer and Scripture reading, we felt at last our ceremony was complete.

What a day it had been, and what a weird beginning to our life together! Some day we'd be telling the whole incredible story to our grandchildren. Weary beyond description, we felt like we had fought a battle and won. We looked to the future with joy and hope, knowing that the Lord loved us and we were in His care.

In the days and weeks following my ordeal and escape, newspapers all over the country carried the story. What had been untouchable before it was confirmed by the police now became sensational news. One Boston paper, greedy for attention-grabbing headlines, ran the caption, "Cult member kidnapped!" This really grieved and upset all of us at Jews for Jesus. It's untruthful and misleading to the public for the media to classify Jews for Jesus as a cult along with the questionable "isms" of these times. Jews for Jesus is a straight Bible-believing, interdenominational group that works hand-in-hand with established evangelical churches. All their members belong to sound, Christ-honoring congregations. Our only distinction is that we believe we can still honor our ethnic and cultural heritage as Jews while believing in Christ as Lord and Savior.

My parents think that Jews for Jesus has some weird hold on me. No one has a hold on me except Jesus Himself. I came to faith in Him before I started attending Jews for Jesus Bible studies. Jews for Jesus didn't take anything away from me, they helped me to appreciate more than ever my being Jewish.

My faith and allegiance are not in or to any organization, or person, but in Christ as Messiah of Israel and Savior of the whole world. Even while I was outwardly going along with the deprogrammers, deep down inside I knew I had not trusted Jesus in vain. For two years I saw prayers answered, had peace and joy in my heart, and a relationship with God. These things no one could take away from me, though they might force me through physical and emotional duress to say things I didn't mean. No one can brainwash from a man's heart what God has planted there.

I believe that God kept me safe and delivered me from my ordeal because Christian friends all over the country were praying for me. I know that He has forgiven me for denying Him, even as He forgave Peter. I know He gave Christine and me our love for one another, and it's right for us to be together.

Two weeks after our strange little wedding in Reno, our new San Francisco Jews for Jesus friends held a wedding reception for us at the headquarters building. Together Chris and I stood under the traditional Jewish wedding canopy and repeated our committment to one another. This time Moishe Rosen, a fully ordained minister, presided. Christine, with flowers in her hair, wore the long white dress again. Our friends worked hard to make the occasion the kind of celebration we will always remember with joy. From the home baked and decorated three-tiered wedding cake, to each special Jewish delicacy on the table and each flower arrangement, the reception was a labor of love. The only thing that marred our happiness at the reception was the knowledge that my parents couldn't share that joy.

I still love my parents very much, and I hope they know that. I realize, too, that they love me; there was never any doubt in my mind about that. But, as sometimes happens, their love was misguided, possessive, and overprotective. I understand that in a strange way my kidnapping and deprogramming represented their love, care, and concern. At no time during my ordeal did I ever allow my frustration over the situation to turn to hatred for my parents, because I knew they felt they had to do what they did.

Most Jewish people wouldn't go to such extremes as my parents and the deprogrammers did in order to bring back a family member to their idea of the truth. Nevertheless I hope those who read this story will bear no animosity toward my parents. I have forgiven them, and I'm praying that one day they will understand the truth about Jesus and know God's forgiveness, too.

If only my parents could have known the Lord and all He has done for me! If only they could have allowed themselves to know Christine better, to see in her all the good and godly qualities she possesses; if only they had realized how much she was ready to love them and how much she wanted their acceptance, the whole thing would not have happened.

Almost as distressing as the actual kidnapping and deprogramming experience was my parents' denial that it had ever happened. After interviewing my parents, and their friends *Time* Magazine inferred in their news story that I was unstable mentally and that I had made up the whole story. My integrity, my testimony, and my sanity were put in question because of that denial. In a way that was as much a part of the whole nightmare as were the physical and emotional abuses I suffered.

The matter was not concluded just because I was finally free. Because the law was involved, the state had to press charges, and I would have to testify. I knew that I didn't have any choice if I were to be honest before God and man. Still, the thought of facing my parents in a courtroom and speaking facts against them that could result in their imprisonment caused me much agony and despair.

From the very outset, I was tempted to refuse to testify for the sake of my family. Moishe Rosen and I discussed this, and he told me that it was my duty to go to the trial and give testimony unless my parents willingly admitted the facts of my abduction. I could see that Moishe was right. If only my father would tell the truth in court! I prayed he would, but it seemed almost too much to hope for.

For weeks before the scheduled trial date, all of our friends at the Jews for Jesus prayer meetings were praying for Christine and me, for my family's welfare, and for a reconcilation between us. I knew that reconciliation would be impossible unless my parents could admit they had done this thing to me and wanted my forgiveness. They could only consider my offer of forgiveness an insult if they still felt they had acted properly toward me. I desperately wanted to forgive them, to be reconciled, and to gain their acceptance of Christine as my wife. Could they change their attitude? It would certainly take a miracle. The day Christine and I boarded our plane to attend the hearing at Newton District Court, we were still praying for that miracle.

The night before the hearing I met with Assistant District Attorney Elizabeth Fahey and Herman Tarnow, a New York attorney who had previously handled some Jews for Jesus matters in New York City. This time he was there solely to represent me, and yet also to protect my parents from a harsh penalty if at all possible. They had suffered enough already from magazine and newspaper exposure. Mr. Tarnau suggested that justice would be served sufficiently if my father would admit in court that the events that I described had really transpired with his knowledge and consent. We all doubted that my father could bring himself to admit that, but we hoped he would. The only alternative was that the state would prosecute, and my father would risk being convicted of a felony. If that happened, at the very least he would lose his government employment, and it could entail actual imprisonment. In answer to all our prayers, my father did acknowledge that the whole thing really happened, and he agreed to sign a sworn statement to that effect.

The next morning I took the stand and told Newton District Court Judge Monte Basbas that I was prepared to withdraw the charges because I didn't want to testify against my father. When he asked me why, I told him, "There's been an acknowledgement of the facts in this case. That is satisfactory to me, and I want to reconcile with my father."

The state attorney and the judge and the police force were all satisfied with that resolution of the case. It was the least painful solution to a very uncomfortable situation.

Afterwards, there were hugs and kisses all around, but things were still rather tense. Mr. Tarnow spoke to my mother outside the courtroom.

"Mrs. Levitt," he said. "Whatever you might think or feel about Christine, she did one thing that is absolutely the bottom line. She stood by your son through thick and thin. I know many a mother who'd give her eye teeth to have a daughter-in-law who'd stick by her son like that. She's really proven herself. Given every indication that Ken had left her at the altar, she didn't give up. She stood by him and was supportive. She found herself in *Time* Magazine the day after she was married. How much more of a test of courage does a person need? You can be proud of her and respect her courage and loyalty. I'm not asking you to act happy and carefree as though nothing had happened, but you can try to realize that this woman really stood by your son in a time of need."

My mother looked at Mr. Tarnow thoughtfully. "You know, it's all very difficult," she said, as she turned to go back where everyone was gathering to leave.

My mother walked over to Christine and hugged her. "Thank you very much for all you've done," she told Chris. We were all crying, and I could see the barriers beginning to crumble.

Appendix 1

If You Were To Be Deprogrammed

By Moishe Rosen

A self-styled task force of wolves in sheep's clothing has taken upon itself what it considers to be a mission of mercy. These are the "deprogrammers," a group comprised mostly of concerned parents and religious Jews who seek by nefarious methods to destroy the faith of young Jewish believers in Christ. Many of these deprogrammers actually believe that Jews who believe in Jesus are emotionally unsound and that those who try to dissuade them from their beliefs are doing the work of God. They justify their methods by treating Jewish faith in Christ as a mental and social abberation. There is a vital need for both Gentile and Jewish Christians to be educated and warned about these deprogrammers so that they can deal intelligently and effectively with this insidious threat.

How the Deprogrammers Operate

Separation. The deprogrammers operate on familiar principles. First, the parents of the prospective subject visit the believer and say they would like to be alone with their son or daughter. They invite the believer for a drive or a meal. Once in the car or home, the believer is "kidnapped," and taken to a group of deprogrammers in alien, totally unfamiliar surroundings, often a motel room. The strategy is that the deprogrammers separate the believer from his fellow believers and place him in an unfamiliar situation. In order to do their "work," the deprogrammers must first disorient and intimidate their subject. For this reason they usually don't work with the believer in his parents' home, because the familiarity of those surroundings would serve to remind him of his own identity enough for him to be able to maintain his orientation.

The deprogrammers claim that it is important for them to separate the young believer from his religious community because the Christian leaders or elders have some unusual power over the person. This may be the case in a cult situation, but of course it doesn't hold true in a normal church relationship. In any case, separation from all strong believers is imperative for the deprogrammers' plan, since supportive fellowship of any kind would thwart their purposes.

The deprogrammers agree that one of the first steps in the deprogramming process is to separate the believer from his Bible. Although the deprogrammers sometimes pose as true believers, this approach immediately uncovers their true identity and purpose. Imposed spiritual starvation is never to be regarded as a holy imperative, for the Scripture teaches that we are to consider the Word of God as essential food for nourishment, (I Tim. 3:15, 16).

The Attack Approach. This tactic is not new. It has been used effectively in military spheres for centuries to acquire information from an unwilling prisoner, or to restructure loyalties. In modern language we call it "brain washing." Human beings are creatures with limitations, and in order to achieve the desired results, the deprogrammers have only to attack until they reach the limits of the individual's endurance. The deprogrammers proudly claim that their methods are one hundred percent effective. Nevertheless, as in the foregoing incident, captured Christians have escaped, sometimes with their faith temporarily shaken, but not destroyed.

It's easy for the deprogrammers to trip up even a Christian with this attack approach. In the deprogramming process there are usually six to ten deprogrammers surrounding the believer, sometimes many more. These people eat and sleep normally, while the believer is often deprived of food, granted a bare minimum of sleep, and subjected to a great deal of harassment.

As believers, we have the holy obligation to confess our faith. Therefore, the deprogrammers' questions seem at first like welcome opportunities to share the faith. They ask, "What do you believe,?" "How did you come to believe this?" "Could you explain to us why you believe?" What Christian could resist such an opportunity? But the Bible admonishes us to be wise as serpents and not to address ourselves to insincere questions.

When a Christian gives his testimony, it is to proclaim the grace and mercy of God in light of his own particular unworthiness regarding salvation. Often the believer will describe a certain problem from which the Lord delivered him. If a person has had a problem of indulgence in dope, degraded sex, or a certain kind of pride, the deprogrammers might reintroduce this to the believer. Pride is the easiest stumbling block, as the Bible warns us. Pride tells us that we "deserve" something. If the deprogrammers can get the subject hooked into a pride trip, then they can get him hooked on almost any old habit (Proverbs 16:18). The Christian in such a situation must remember that he is bought with a price and doesn't deserve any kind of self indulgence.

Guilt. Another prime tactic the deprogrammers use is the appeal to a young believer's love for his parents, combined with his susceptibility to guilt feelings. Most people have at one time or another done things, or displayed attitudes towards their parents for which they are genuinely sorry. Since all Christian teaching points to the necessity for love and restitution, the young believer is eager to become the child he feels his parents expect him to be. This good motive is used by the deprogrammers as a lever to increase the believer's guilt feelings. In this early state, the parents or the deprogrammers appeal to the believer that for the sake of his family, he ought to sever his relationship with the particular fellowship of believers from which he has been kidnapped. The deprogrammers don't at first ask the believer to renounce Christ, but that is only steps away. Few can resist this technique, and once the believer has accepted the deprogrammers and parents as his friends, who only have his "best interests at heart," it's just a matter of time until he succumbs and reaches their intended conclusion. The deprogrammers have all the time in the world. They will work on a person for days, however long it takes.

Renunciation. Toward the end of the deprogramming, when the subject is broken in spirit, the deprogrammers goad him into performing some act of renunciation. This act may be to slander the names of the people he knew, especially the elders or the minister of the fellowship or church. In some cases, it might be something more unspeakable, such as cursing the name of Jesus, or spitting on the Bible. Once the person has done something of that magnitude, the deprogrammers remind him of how difficult it would be to return to the fellowship he attended, and often they convince him that he has committed an "unpardonable sin."

How Can We Anticipate Deprogramming?

We must expect that many parents will be very receptive to the idea of cooperating with deprogrammers to "free" their victimized children from the "Jesus trip." They will provide all necessary funds and go to great lengths to accomplish the desired end, but there is much that God would have us do to prepare for such a possibility.

The Word of God. Every believer requires the consumption and digestion of the Word of God for spiritual sustenance. Bible memory work is imperative to strengthen a person against the threat of being deprogrammed. The deprogrammers may take away your Bible, but they can't take away your memory. Furthermore, knowledge of the Bible must exist on an independent basis. That is, it must stem from private thought and study, not group teaching. Too much of our Bible "knowledge" is made up of predigested conclusions based on what our particular group of believers assumes. A believer should always be able to back up his faith with Scripture. Know why you believe what you believe.

Forgiveness. Remember that there is no act that can be committed that will take a believer out of salvation and away from God if he truly repents and wants to have the Lord. Where there is repentance, there is always forgiveness. It is the responsibility of the elders in Christ to teach new believers the depth and extent of Christ's forgiveness. One of the tactics used by the deprogrammers is to convince the "broken" victim that his renunciation or slander of his fellowship or testimony is too great a sin to be forgiven by his old friends. They convince him that it will be no use ever to try to reinstate himself into that fellowship. We must remember that the blood of Christ can cleanse us from ALL unrighteousness if we confess our sins to the Father. Likewise, as brothers and sisters in Christ, we, too, should be quick to show forgiveness to one who has stumbled. Remember, no one is saved because of what he deserves. God is the one who pieces us into the body of Christ, and it is His grace that will keep us there.

Emotions. Don't allow love for any person to be used as a lever against your faith. The parents of the deprogramming victims often try to appeal to their emotions by saying, "If you really love us, then come away where we can sit together and talk." The believer will usually comply, because he wants to do all he can to show his love and respect for his parents' wishes. New Christians should be instructed that there is a point at which they should not allow their love to be used in this way.

Also, there is a time to witness, and a time not to witness. The time not to witness is in a situation contrived by someone who doesn't want to hear, but rather wants to dissuade the believer from his faith. Conditioned to be harmless as doves, we, as Christians, sometimes forget to be also as wise as serpents. We must be prepared to keep our emotions from endangering us or our brothers and sisters in Christ. A good idea when being approached by a parent or other family member in this way is to take along another believer. There's safety in numbers.

Humility. Christian faith is not a rational process by which a believer comes to a logical conclusion that Jesus is Lord. Faith is a gift from God whereby we believe that which the natural man is incapable of believing: spiritual truth. There is much to learn about our faith, and God has given us all eternity to grow in understanding and wisdom. Therefore, a new believer should realize that just because he may not have an answer to a question, that is no reason to think that there is no answer. To think that at any point you must be able to come up with perfect answers to a person's questions is to fall into the trap of pride. Never let yourself believe that you know everything that is in the Bible and everything that God has inferred in His Word. Above all, don't confuse paradoxes with contradictions when examining Scripture. A believer should be humble enough to allow a great margin for the things he doesn't understand, and faith-filled enough to believe that God is making him into the kind of person who can and will be trusted with more and more spiritual insight.

How To Deal with the Enemy

The deprogrammers, no matter how convinced they may be that they are doing God a service, are the enemies of your soul. If encountered by such people, here are some recommendations on handling the situation.

Cooperation. NEVER talk to someone and try to persuade him while you are being held against your will. Only a free man can talk and think straight. You have to be able to eat when you want, sleep when you want, and have the right of privacy and the choice to leave or stay. Just the fact that you're being held against your will is enough to interfere with your being able to think clearly and to comprehend.

Different groups of deprogrammers allow the victim varying degrees of freedom, but in some cases it has been reported that the parents themselves actually slept across the threshold or doorway of a room in order to prevent the possibility of escape. Often the deprogrammers count on the fact that most people, especially Christians, prefer to avoid making a scene. The victims, being in unfamiliar territory and often without money in their pockets, are apt to decide that cooperation is the best way to meet the situation. DO NOT BE COOPERATIVE! Tell anyone who is holding you that you are being held against your will, and you refuse to talk to them.

Deprogrammer Ted Patrick was once quoted in *Time* Magazine as saying, "If I can get them communicating, I can always win. I say, 'Prove you are a Christian.' This shows up the person's own frailties." Don't accept any kindness from the deprogrammers, and don't communicate with them. Accept the fact that anyone who would interfere with your walk with God in this way is your enemy. Soldiers in wartime are taught not to communicate with the enemy. If captured, they are to state only their name, rank, and serial number. You, too, can refuse to talk. Some of this deprogramming is demonic—Remember to resist the devil and he will flee.

Prayer. Talk to Jesus within yourself, but don't let your captors hear you. Remember the promises of God in Scripture and recite verses to yourself. Dwell on past experiences of answered prayer. Don't let the deprogrammers get into your mind. Don't reveal to them what you're thinking, except to express resistance. To keep your mind busy, recite poetry to yourself, or count the cracks in the floor or ceiling. DO NOT OPEN UP.

Fasting. Another effective technique that has been used to defeat the deprogrammers is to go on an extended fast, which the captors interpret as a hunger strike. Such a fast, accompanied by prayer, is actually strengthening under these circumstances, and it puts the moral responsibility for the consequences on the captors. If the captive can find the strength from God to maintain absolute silence, physical passivity to violence, and complete refusal to ingest either food or water, the chances of his being released soon are much better. In that situation, you should remember to continue your refusal to eat and drink and remain absolutely passively uncooperative until you are away from the deprogrammers and back to complete safety. Otherwise, the deprogrammers might trick you into eating or dinking or communicating with them by saying they have decided to let you go. This happened to someone who was being held, where his captors said they were releasing him. They stopped the car in a gas station and someone brought cokes to the car. The victim drank one, whereupon the deprogrammers, no longer worried about his becoming dehydrated, refused to release him and continued their harassment.

Dealing with Physical Violence. The main tool that the deprogrammers use is psychological duress, but sometimes they try to induce this by physical violence or the threat of physical violence. Then they resort to kicking, slapping, and shoving the victim in order to intimidate him. In one bizarre case, a girl was repeatedly raped and tortured and told that her religion made her subhuman. Serious physical attack of this kind is rare. Nevertheless, should the victim encounter any degree of physical violence, it's best just to go limp. Don't make the mistake of thinking of yourself as a martyr for the faith, because such pride works against you.

The best way to endure physical violence is to remember that it is not directed against you as a person, but against Christ who is in you. Separate the physical pain from the psychological pain. Don't allow yourself to be shocked if you are slapped, shoved, or slammed up against a wall. One way to handle the pain is to compare in your heart what you are enduring to the agony Christ suffered at Calvary. In the light of His sufferings, almost any pain seems small and insignificant by comparison.

It's very important that you don't shove back, scream, or respond in any manner. If you were to fight back, your captors would consider that justification for further acts of violence. God built the human body in such a way that if the physical pain becomes too great to bear, a person loses consciousness. Remember that He will not tempt you above that which you are able to bear, but will, with the testing, make a way of escape for you. (I Cor. 10:13). If pain is happening to you, He has already given you the strength to bear it and to endure.

Humiliation. Part of the intimidation process is humiliation. The deprogrammers might hold their victim in such confines that he cannot tend to his personal toilet or relieve himself. This is extremely embarrassing to most people. One person broke during deprogramming when he wasn't allowed the use of a bathroom. When he could no longer contain himself and defecated, the deprogrammers made him sit in his own filth. This humiliated and embarrassed him to the point of tears. If you ever find yourself in such an embarrassing or humiliating situation, remember that a believer who has been cleansed by Christ cannot be defiled by any bodily function over which he has no control. Only the thoughts of his heart can defile him.

Accusations of Insanity. While being held, you might encounter a statement like this: "We think you're insane. If you'll just talk to us and show us that you're a reasonable person, we won't have you committed to a mental institution." Denying insanity won't work, because insane people never admit to being insane. Remember, anyone can be driven insane by pressure tactics and the withholding of bodily necessities like food and sleep. Do *not* try to manipulate the deprogrammers. They are not bound by Christian ethics. They have only one job to do, and that is to get you to renounce your faith at all costs. Never fake insanity as a means of escape, because they might have you committed to a mental institution. While being held, never take any medication from anyone purporting to be a doctor.

Escape. One article about deprogrammers reports that a number of abductees have managed to escape through windows. One girl said that she felt they were going to kill her anyway, and that it was worth the risk of jumping. Don't do anything foolhardy, but do try to escape. If you succeed, go to the police and tell them that you have been held against your will. Volunteer to take a battery of tests that comprise a legal sanity hearing on which to base your case. If you can't find police, go to a nearby church and report what has happened to you. Try to call your pastor or Christian friends collect, and seek their help.

It's not wrong to go to the police. We have been conditioned not to complain against parents. But when parents declare that they will stop at nothing to get their sons and daughters to renounce their faith, then those sons and daughters must, at all costs, protect themselves, their personal freedom, and particularly the future freedom of others.

Capsule Advice to Deprogramming Victims. If captured by deprogrammers, behave like a prisoner of war. You must fight the deprogrammers all the way, as though they were going to kill you. Remember to resist but remain passive. When you are confronted with what seems like a monolithic force, you can be be brought to the point of believing anything. But remember, as a Christian, stronger is He that is in you than he that is in the world.

The law is now being brought into question concerning some of the deplorable tactics of the deprogrammers. Every person has the right to freedom of religion and freedom of choice. Furthermore, as creatures of God, we should demand and expect the same kind of choice from the world that we have received from the Lord. Jesus said, "Behold, I stand at the door and knock." God does not abduct His children!

In conclusion, there is no "cure" for a real case of Christianity. The deprogrammers will never be one hundred percent effective, because the experience of knowing Christ keeps on in a person even when he has been brought low. Keep in mind the disciple Peter who denied the Lord three times, saying, "I never knew him." Peter came back to become the strongest of the apostles. The Lord can always forgive and reinstate His children and accomplish through each one what He has purposed to do. Remember the promises of God in Christ!

Never give anyone up to the deprogrammers. A few might actually renounce the Lord under extreme pressure; yet there is the probability that if they do, they will still repent and come back. And when someone returns to Christ after such an ordeal, treat him with a double measure of welcome and rejoicing, like the "prodigal son."

Appendix 2

An Appeal to Christian Friends

By Moishe Rosen

In recent years God has been doing an unusual work among the Jewish people, so that many Jews have been responding to the Gospel call. Being Jewish and serving Jesus has never been easy, but we have found that God gives us the strength to endure the disapproval of our fellow Jews and to enjoy our salvation and abundant life in Christ.

In the days immediately ahead, we expect to see a great turning of Jewish people to Christ, and subsequent distress on the part of their families who might misunderstand. Ken Levitt's story is remarkable because of the extremes to which his parents went. Nevertheless, as Christ is becoming increasingly attractive to Jews, and as the Lost Sheep of the House of Israel begin to heed the beckoning call of the Good Shepherd, we expect to see more of this type of violent reaction. The Jews who believe in Jesus need a greater measure of understanding from their non-Jewish brothers and sisters in Christ. But most of all, we need for Gentile believers to love our fellow Jews, even in incidents such as this deprogramming. Help us to show Christian love and respect to our non-Christian families and community, that the whole world might see that the love of Christ truly is invincible.

As a group, Jews for Jesus is not only committed to proclaiming the Gospel, but we are also committed to sharing the burden with those Jews who suffer for the sake of naming Christ as Savior. We are happy to stand with Jews or others who might need such strength as we can give. We welcome inquiries and offer assistance to those in such times of distress as experienced by Ken Levitt. Jews for Jesus can be contacted by writing to:

60 Haight Street, San Francisco, CA 94102 or by calling: (415) 864-2600.